EFFECTIVE SCHOOLS WORK

This book is dedicated to the staff and pupils at
Agnes Stewart Church of England High School, Leeds.
Thank you for letting me be part of your journey.

Effective Schools Work

LEE JACKSON
(AND FRIENDS)

KINGSWAY PUBLICATIONS
EASTBOURNE

First published 2003

ISBN 1 84291 082 5

Published by
KINGSWAY COMMUNICATIONS LTD
Lottbridge Drove, Eastbourne BN23 6NT, England.
Email: books@kingsway.co.uk

Book design and production for the publishers by
Bookprint Creative Services, P.O. Box 827, BN21 3YJ, England.
Printed in Great Britain.

Contents

Thanks

Saying thanks always makes me paranoid about forgetting people, but here goes anyway . . .

Thanks to my advisors and contributors – Jon Burns, Simon Hall, Alison Farnell, Pete Gilbert, Amaze, Abi, Sarah, Emma, Dad, Jo Stow, Pastor Bob Fry and Nic Shepard. To Ruth Thomas (SMN) for the email list.

To Baz, 'Lovely' Lenton, Toby, Steve, Justin, Boycey and Acko for keeping me normal.

Steve, Lionel, Andy Lanc and Andy Len, Ruth and the crew at Bridge Street Church – you are living up to your heritage.

To all the teachers who have impacted me over the years – Pat, Graeme, Andy, Hayden, Chris, Richard, Pete, Philip, Stan and many others.

To the Church of Leeds, Together For Leeds and Martin Scott for your positive view of our wonderful pivotal city. And to Transform, LAM, Kidz Klub, Leeds Youth Cell Network and Teen Challenge for doing the business in Leeds. Thanks to the prayer warriors whom I know, and those that I don't – I am nothing without you. Special thanks to Steve, Robin, Geraldine, Ruth, Leslie and Beryl.

To Janet, Robin, Pete and the PE staff at Allerton High: you have always made me feel part of your team (and wine club!) – thanks.

Cheers to Patty and Linda – the two great mature women in my life.

To the LFIS trustees, especially Mike and David – thanks for believing in me.

Thanks to David Brent for helping me become a better manager.

To St Matthias for giving us a home and YFC for letting us hang out. Big up to the Fly boys – Edge, Waaard and James, and the one and only Stu Helm.

Thanks to everyone in Dayspring for supporting Clare and me so well.

To all my friends at Leeds Faith In Schools (and our volunteers): I love you all and I am glad to be part of your lives.

Xtra Big Thanks to Christine – this book would not have happened without your typing skills and patience! I am so glad you are part of our team.

To Billy, Pea and Dooler – I love my girls ☺

And lastly to all the schools that have allowed me and LFIS to be part of their community. Never been a dull moment so far, and I look forward to what's to come.

Preface

33% of the world's population is Christian, and between 1970 and 2000 the growth rate of Christianity in the world was 70,000 a day, or 1.6%.

33% is quoted in *The UK Christian Handbook Religious Trends 2002/2003* and in *Encyclopaedia Britannica*. These figures both excite and frustrate me as we look at the state we are in in the West, but nothing has spurred me on more than a disco I once did as a DJ at one of my schools.

'John'

Meeting this young person changed the way that I do school and youth work. I'd had a long day but went to the school to do the Year 7 disco between 7 and 9 pm. I was pretty exhausted (with twin baby girls at home!) and the last thing I wanted to do was load my car up with speakers and equipment. So I arrived not feeling 'full of the joy of the Lord'. But I went into the hall and started to set things up for my standard two-hour party disco with Macarena and all the other classics. I wanted some of the young people to come and help with the gear so I could hang out with them a bit, and one or two of them asked if they could DJ with me. A young-looking Year 7 (11-year-old) came to help out: he was small, a bit scruffy looking and slightly unwashed. He seemed about half the size of me. We chatted and he drank loads of Coke and ate endless smelly crisps, and I allowed him to put on some CDs. He really enjoyed getting involved. I was putting a CD on ready for the next track when he tapped me on the shoulder and said something which still stays with me today. He said, 'I wish you were my brother.'

It was one of those moments when I didn't know what to do. I had gone with a fairly bad attitude and didn't particularly want to be there, but John was so happy just to be with me for the evening that he said those words to me. I asked about John in school the next day and was told he had a very difficult time at home, and even though he wasn't doing well at school, they kept him there because they felt it was safer for him to be in school than it was for him to be at home.

My just hanging out with him and letting him be a DJ's helper at a school disco made such a difference to him. When he said that he wished I was his brother, half of me wanted to burst into tears and the other half wanted to give him a big hug. It was a complete surprise and I didn't know how to react to it.

God knew what he was doing getting me to do the school disco that night! One comment from a little Year 7 kid affected my life and schools work for ever – far more than any facts and figures ever could, no matter how encouraging they are.

Who Is This Book For?

> If Christianity should happen to be true – that is to say, if its God is the real God of the universe – then defending it may mean talking about anything and everything. Things can be irrelevant to the proposition that Christianity is false, but nothing can be irrelevant to the proposition that Christianity is true. All things not only may have something to do with the Christian God, but must have something to do with Him if He lives and reigns. (G. K. Chesterton)

This book is quite simply for anyone who has contact with schools, both primary and secondary. It's for people like myself who are full-time schools workers through to people who do assemblies once a term, and everyone in between. The advice and research is relevant in a school environment, no matter how much contact you have with school.

I hope it will help to deflate some of the rumours, challenge apparent political correctness and illuminate the 'strange world and institution' that is school. In my time as a schools worker I have been to many different schools and can honestly say that every one is completely unique, but by using some of the principles and practical help in this book, you will be able to act appropriately and be good news to our schools.

If you have a flick through the book, you will notice it does not have long-winded chapters with big theological expositions. This is a practical book giving tips and advice with real stories and genuine accounts of Christians who have been back to school. I have consulted most of the Christian schools workers on the Schools Ministry Network mailing list (see Appendix 2) and been in touch with a lot of my friends. People have helpfully contributed stories, tips and hints, so (thankfully) it is not just from the pen of 'a person in an ivory tower' but I hope encompasses a wide variety of Christian backgrounds and denominations with one common goal – we want to be a help, not a hindrance, to our schools.

Some material is specific to schools work and some is general good youth work practice which will be relevant in and out of the school environment. I must also stress that this is not a book just for younger people: one of the best youth workers I know is 65 years old. Whatever your age, please consider that schools need your help, advice and experience. I will also try to help with some fears and concerns, so that we can become more professional and effective in our contact with schools, however limited.

My good friend Andy has had many obstacles to overcome, including disability and other problems, but despite everything he is the most reliable and valued member of our school team. When I told him I was writing this book he said that I should tell you all, 'If God can use me in school, then he can use you! Don't hesitate to try!'

I have lived and breathed schools work for the last eight years, and want to convey the passion and hope I have for our schools. If you want honest and real advice about schools work of every kind then this book is for you. I have emptied my brain producing it, so please – enjoy!

Lee, Leeds and Leeds Faith In Schools

The backdrop to this book is my journey with Leeds Faith In Schools and the city of Leeds. Here are a few details that will help to put the book into context.

A brief history of Leeds Faith In Schools:

- *March 1993* – Following a high school mission 'Festival '92' led by Steve Chalke of Oasis, David Hawkins, Vicar of St George's, calls a meeting to explore the setting up of permanent schools work in Leeds.
- *March 1994* – Working group set up to develop the vision.
- *June 1994* – Open meeting of Christians across Leeds where proposal for Leeds Faith In Schools is outlined.
- *July 1994* – Trustees, Management Committee and Appeals Co-ordinator appointed.
- *September 1994* – I am appointed as first Leeds Faith In Schools worker. The project is launched for a two-year trial period. We had enough money for one month's wage. I worked in four high schools in Leeds.

- *January 1995* – Janet Gibson is appointed part-time Administrator.
- *July 1995* – Internal evaluation of the pilot project.
- *May 1996* – Leeds Faith In Schools obtains charitable status.
- *April 1997* – Rob Fry is appointed as the second full-time schools worker in Leeds.
- *September 1998* – Nicola Bray is appointed as the third full-time schools worker, supported by Churches Together in Morley, Leeds.
- *April 1999* – A small office is acquired.
- *December 1999* – I am appointed Team Leader / Project Manager.
- *January 2000* – Duncan Stow is appointed as a part-time schools worker in Horsforth School. The following month Isabel Oliveira is appointed as a part-time schools worker, based in Prince Henry's School, Otley.
- *April 2000* – LFIS moves office premises to St Matthias Centre, Burley.
- *May 2000* – Rob leaves the employ of Faith In Schools to become pastor of New Life Church, Rawdon. He remains working with the project as an associate worker.
- *September 2000* – Emma Flint and Sarah Bradford are employed. Sarah is to work in Aireborough, supported largely by Aireborough Churches Together.
- *October 2000* – Ed Baines Clarke and Matt Edge take a year out with the Youth For Christ fly team as basketball coaches with Leeds Faith In Schools.
- *January 2001* – Abi Monteith is appointed to the position of full-time worker in Morley, after Nicola moves on.
- *September 2001* – We employ Christine as a full-time administrator to replace Luisa who started work in 1999

and Matt Edge comes back for a second year as Fly team leader in Leeds with new Fly member James Cleveland.

- *February 2002* – We employ Claire Lancaster to replace Isobel in Otley schools (on the outskirts of Leeds). We also acquire Jo Stow (a local Catholic parish worker), and Fiona Bailey (a children's worker in Rawdon) as associate workers, and a few volunteers from DNA and Transform (year out courses).

Now some information about the city we are based in.

Leeds . . . 'No ordinary city'

- It is the fastest growing city in Europe.
- It is a '24 hour' city.
- It has a branch of Harvey Nichols!
- Leeds has more law and accountancy firms than any-where in Britain outside of London, and is considered the second most powerful city in the UK.
- It just spent £165 million renovating the train station.
- £2.4 billion of property development has been completed since 1991.
- Leeds is the second largest metropolitan district in the UK.
- Leeds employs 12,000 people in media based industries.
- 35% of the nation's internet traffic passes through Leeds, and there are more high speed internet lines per head of population in Leeds than any other major city.

But . . .

- It is known as a 'two-tier' city and came 338 out of 376 local authorities ranked in order of 'quality of life' based on factors such as unemployment, crime and average income.

- Large areas of Leeds are still among the most deprived in the country.
- Leeds is known as the 'the child abuse capital of Britain'.
- There are over 168,000 young people in Leeds. Many of them and their parents have never had any contact with church. We estimate there are not much more than 300 Christian young people in Leeds.
- Leeds has around half the national average of church attendance.

Thankfully, though, I and a lot of Christians around the country love it! We are strategising and praying for it like mad.

Now some information about myself.

Lee

I was born in 1970 in Billingham in the north east of England where I lived until I was twelve years old. Moving to Leeds in 1988, I got a job in a solicitor's and then moved on to work in the Crown Court and the County Court.

I was also doing youth work at St Barnabas Church in Leeds and I had formed the band HOG (House of God) with Nick Mawby and Justin Thomas. We were the first ever British Christian rap (hip-hop) group, and travelled doing festivals and even went abroad once or twice. We connected with the World Wide Message Tribe in Manchester and were their support act for a couple of years, and I still DJ with them now.

In 1993 I decided to leave my job in the courts to do a discipleship training course (DTS) with YWAM (Youth with a Mission) in sunny St Helens in Merseyside, and an urban ministry course which I did for five months before moving to Northern Ireland outreach-working in a staunch loyalist environment followed by work in a Catholic environment.

While away at YWAM, I had a telephone call from Doreen McConnell, a Scripture Union contact from Leeds, who had been praying for a schools worker in Leeds for several years. Even a city the size of Leeds, with three quarters of a million people, had no Christian schools work to speak of and we really wanted to set something up fast. So she asked me if I wanted a job that didn't exist, and I said, 'That sounds great – what is a schools worker?' I started on 1 September 1994 as the first ever full-time schools worker in Leeds.

Since then I have worked with Leeds Faith In Schools, continuing with HOG (until 1996) and always DJing in some shape or form. Now I run www.2turntables.co.uk, a network of Christian and 'not-yet Christian' DJs who train, pray and network with each other in the dance music scene. I do DJ workshops with young people and all the other things that schools workers do. I am a keen basketball player, although not a very good one, being only 5'9"! We also had the Youth for Christ Fly basketball team in Leeds. This was a dream of mine (and Jon Burns') for years.

Clare and I have twin daughters, and go to Dayspring Church in Leeds.

1

A Young Person's World Today

Here are a few 'snapshots' I found that help to explain why young people are like they are!

They are often known as the millennium generation or Generation Y. Generation Y is currently under 18 years old, born in 1984 or later. They are participants in what Dean Borgman calls 'the second great watershed' in youth culture (*Christianity* magazine, February 1997). And the repercussions are causing us to rethink how churches do youth ministry. The first watershed, Borgman says, took place in the forties, when the concept of 'youth culture' was born. Following the Depression and World War II, and in conjunction with the advancement of the industrial age, a harvest of young people crashed onto the scene with free time and extra money.

They are also known as the mosaic generation, and *Quadrant* magazine (September 2001) described them in the following way.

When tiles are found in an archaeological dig they are normally scattered in the earth and have to be put back together correctly to reform the picture. The mosaic generation are used to taking pieces of information from a wide variety of sources and putting them into a single worldview. Their main characteristic is focusing on a part, without any sense of the underlying time frame . . . events are pieces of a historical mosaic but are divorced from the world view (or meta narrative as it is sometimes called) that goes with it. To them Jesus is just another piece of the mosaic alongside Buddha or somebody else.

Other features of Generation Y include:

- They use a computer much more naturally than their parents and they are good at it too. They communicate through text messaging.
- They have and expect to have sexual experience with several partners as a norm while still at school.
- They have teachers despairing how to control them let alone teach them.
- They or their friends start a family when under the legal age for intercourse. Britain still has the highest rate of teenage pregnancy in Europe.
- They are the first generation to have little sense of the spiritual as Christian and thus leave the church in large numbers finding it totally irrelevant to their way of life.
- They are the first generation to be taught right and wrong but not to be taught good and evil, the consequence of the previous generation's abandonment of absolute truth.

Absolute truth is something that as Christians we take for granted. I believe the truth is that Jesus died and rose again, but there has been an erosion in the acceptance of absolute truth over the last 20 years or so which means that people believe in 'a series of truths' instead. For example, people will save trees and fight to save the whales but are happy to have abortions almost as a contraceptive. It has been said the only things that will not be tolerated in society are intolerance and the abuse of children. Does that now mean that everything else is acceptable or justifiable if my belief system fits it?

'The next generation will base who they are on what we tell them.' (Anita Roddick)

The main issue, I believe, for Generation Y is the enormous and intense peer pressure they experience in order to conform with clothing, music, leisure activities, attitudes and relationships. Do not underestimate the power of peer pressure!

It is helpful to ask the question 'What do young people want?'

1. They want to be valued and respected. Watch the film *Never Been Kissed* with Drew Barrymore, where she goes back to her old school as a 28-year-old and has to re-live the horror of bullying and not being part of the 'in crowd' in the school environment.

2. They want real and simple relationships. You only have to watch *The Jerry Springer Show* to understand how complicated people's lives are, and it seems to me that if people just know who their dad is, who their mum is, who their friends are and who their enemies are, that makes life a lot easier.

3. They want a sense of purpose. In the film *Jerry McGuire*, Jerry was a sports agent who couldn't sleep one night and decided to write a paper about how he wanted the business and his life to go. It was all about valuing and showing respect to the people he represented. He photocopied the report in the middle of the night and gave it out to everyone in the company, who applauded him but all quietly agreed that the next day

he was going to be sacked. Is there any surprise why 'The Vision' from www.24-7prayer.com has become so popular as an anthem for young people? (See Appendix 5.) It simply says that we have purpose in Jesus and if you want to be valued, respected and have genuine relationships then he is the person who can help.

Millennials say about themselves:

- My generation seems oblivious.
- Everybody is too feeble because everything's handed to us.
- We don't do anything; we don't have any great achievements.
- We feel like everything is changing and we have nothing to do with it, so we sit back and let it happen.
- No one's thinking for him/herself anymore.
- No one has any sense of honour anymore.
- We have nothing stable to grasp; no one to look up to; no one to believe in.
- We're just coasting.
- We're not standing for anything.
- We desperately need to be standing for something.

'Youth would be an ideal state if it came later in life.' (*The Observer*, 1923)

The entertainment/rally model of youth ministry spawned a generation of great Christian leaders, but teens today aren't looking for Saturday night amusement. 'We have a completely different landscape in which to minister,' says Wayne Rice, founder of Youth Specialties and director of

Understanding Your Teenager. 'The family was intact in those days. Today youth ministry is more like the emergency room in a hospital.' Mark Senter, Chairman of the Christian Education Department at Trinity Evangelical Divinity School, adds: 'We aren't going to be able to do the same things. We have to change!' (From *Christianity Today* magazine.)

2

Relationships, Relationships, Relationships!

After three years, LFIS finally had enough money to employ a second schools worker – very exciting for me, the famous Lone Ranger! When the applications came in we sifted through them in the normal way, but one application stood out from the rest. It was not on the typed form like all the others. It was a colourful creative C.V. with photos and info crammed into its badly photocopied pages. As I glanced through it, there was a phrase that stuck out and persuaded me that we had found our next worker. It said: 'All youth work is based on the three Rs – Relationships, Relationships, Relationships!'

'Right at the heart of God, relationships are key.'

What a statement! Our relationships with our partner, children, family and friends are the most important things in our lives. Last but not least there is our relationship with God. God is 'three in one' so right at the heart of God, relationships are key. When Jesus came to earth he spent his time with a few rough men and women, trying to build relationships with them and make a difference in their lives. He

27

could have chosen instead to ride on a cloud or live as a hermit – you can after all choose to be anything if you are God!

To move toward deeper relationships with people we need to develop a greater sense of honesty and realness. I used to work in the Crown Court in Leeds as an admin officer, shuffling paper from one side of my desk to the other. In the mornings there used to be a ritual that drove me mad. It was the 'say hello to everyone game'. Everyone used to say 'Hello, good morning, how are you?' No one ever replied honestly or ever listened for a reply! 'Yeah, fine thanks' 'Fair to middling' were typical responses. Some people even answered the question when you hadn't asked them! I love giving people more information than they want, so I would answer, 'Well I feel bit tired actually, I am concerned about my relationship with my wife and my dog has got fleas.' You have never seen people run so fast.

I coach and play basketball at school and spent a considerable time with one group of sixth formers, who formed a team a few years ago, playing basketball with them, organising trips, breaking up fights at their parties and just hanging out with them over the summer holidays. Now they have left school they still keep in touch and some of them even train with my team now, which is great. All the time I spent getting them back together and checking if they were all right has paid off with, I hope, friendships for many years to come. No, they are not all sold out, born again Christians, but I have a special friendship with some of them and they are not embarrassed to be seen with 'that bloke who did the religious assemblies'.

But what happens if people don't like you? I used to be in a men's basketball team where most of them seemed to hate me! I left in the end because of this. I had been a faithful member of the team but for whatever reason they loved it when I missed a shot, or got fouled – it was weird. Then I read a bit from the Bible that freaked me out:

> Through us, he brings knowledge of Christ. Everywhere we go, people breathe in the exquisite fragrance. Because of Christ, we give off a sweet scent rising to God, which is recognized by those on the way of salvation – an aroma redolent with life. But those on the way to destruction treat us more like the stench from a rotting corpse. This is a terrific responsibility. Is anyone competent to take it on? No – but at least we don't take God's Word, water it down, and then take it to the streets to sell it cheap. We stand in Christ's presence when we speak; God looks us in the face. We get what we say straight from God and say it as honestly as we can. Does it sound like we're patting ourselves on the back, insisting on our credentials, asserting our authority? Well, we're not. Neither do we need letters of endorsement, either to you or from you. You yourselves are all the endorsement we need. Your very lives are a letter that anyone can read by just looking at you. Christ himself wrote it – not with ink, but with God's living Spirit; not chiseled into stone, but carved into human lives – and we publish it. (2 Corinthians 2:14–17 *The Message*)

Maybe I was the smell of death to these blokes. (Or maybe they just hated me!) These verses have stayed with me as a reminder of what a responsibility we have to try to maintain good relationships with all people, but sometimes, as Jesus taught, you just have to 'shake the dust from your feet and move on'. I do believe this is a last and not a first response, however. Once you get a taste of real relationships in and out of church life there is no going back. Anonymous meetings and shallow friendships stick out like a sore thumb when you have seen and experienced glimpses of the real thing. The emergence in recent years of cell (small group) church is very exciting and I want it desperately to work, especially for young people, as it is probably our last hope of truly reaching and keeping a lost people group.

Note: sections of this chapter have been taken from my book *Dead Men Walking* (Kingsway, 2002).

3

Why Bother With Schools?

Amazingly many Christians and church leaders are still asking this question, perhaps because of fear or a bad experience.

Churches used to be at the centre of the community. The parish church really did serve the parish fully, with all its physical and spiritual needs, and people were 'hatched, matched and despatched' from local churches. But the fact is that, on the whole, the church is not the centre of the community any more. The building may only be open for two hours on Sundays and it may only have one other meeting during the week.

So what are the centres of community life now? Of course it depends on where you live, but it seems to me that I can't think of anything better than schools to fit the bill in our changing society. I genuinely believe that schools are the centre of our fragmented communities; people have to pick their kids up from school and so they meet at the school gates. Some great evangelistic work is done here as people gossip the gospel or invite friends to their Saturday morning Kidz Klubs. See Appendix 2. So if Christians really want to make an impact on the lives of young people then school is a good place to start!

If we are not meaningfully involved in schools then we will be missing our culture as a whole. (Andy Hickford, *Meltdown in Schools*, Stapleford Centre)

Several years ago I had a conversation with a group of churches in Morley, on the south side of Leeds. They invited me to come over and talk to them because they had literally *no* young people in their churches. They asked me how they could reach young people, and there were of course a thousand answers to that, but a simple and effective place to start was in the schools. As a result, a schools worker was appointed in Morley.

Schools organisations were quoting figures on their publicity a few years ago which said that 98 per cent of young people go to school, and on average each of them will spend 15,000 hours in school! Schools need to become more a part of the strategy of local churches who are looking to impact their community.

Matthew 28:19–20 says

Go to the people of all nations and make them my disciples. Baptise them in the name of the Father, the Son, and the Holy Spirit and teach them to do everything I have told you. I will be with you always, even until the end of the world. (Contemporary English Version)

The key word in that sentence is 'go' and, as churches and youth workers are realising, we seem to have had a policy of 'in drag' and not 'outreach'. Jesus didn't tell us to stay in our churches and put on a good event twice a year. The funny thing is that when we talk about 'go' we think about a missionary going to the developing world to impact lives over there, when actually the word 'go' might mean 200 yards to our local primary school or half a mile to our local secondary school. We are still going in the name of Jesus and we are being Jesus to the young people in that community.

Pete Greig (the founder of 24-7 Prayer and a church planter from Revelation Church, Chichester) says that we need 'cultural presence' not 'cultural relevance'. I chewed on that for quite a while and realised schools have their own cultures, their own idiosyncrasies and foibles. As schools workers we are part of the school make-up, but at the same time we are still distinctly different, and that really is the call of the gospel to a disciple of Jesus – to be present not just relevant.

Pete goes on to say, 'It is actually bodies that model the gospel and not just brains.' In other words it is us. It's real people walking around being the hands and feet of Jesus, rather than just an intellectual connection between two people. Of course people can connect brain-to-brain, but young people in school need to see Christianity lived out, not just spoken about.

Part of our philosophy for schools work at Leeds Faith In Schools is that we say we aim to be valued regular visitors not occasional guests. In other words, we're not usually there full-time because we often work in two or three schools, but we are there for a significant amount of time so that the young people can actually connect with us. They know when we are going to be around, and that just makes a difference as we try to be culturally present in schools, which are a microcosm of the society that we live in.

The apostle Paul speaks of this in 1 Corinthians 9:19–22:

> I am not anyone's slave. But I have become a slave to every-
> one, so that I can win as many people as possible. When I am
> with the Jews, I live like a Jew to win Jews. They are ruled
> by the Law of Moses, and I am not. But I live by the Law to
> win them. And when I am with people who are not ruled by
> the Law, I forget about the Law to win them. Of course, I
> never really forget about the law of God. In fact, I am ruled
> by the law of Christ. When I am with people whose faith is
> weak, I live as they do to win them. I do everything I can
> to win everyone I possibly can. (Contemporary English
> Version)

Paul is talking about relevance and presence in this
passage. In order to reach Jewish people he sometimes
had to celebrate their festivals, eat like them, live with
them and spend lots of time chatting with them in
homes and synagogues. He had to be culturally present
not just relevant. And if we can take that as a basis
for what we do in school (or any other youth work),
I really believe it will make us more effective in our
work.

Paul was obviously different from the people that he
reached, but he was still acceptable to them. Phil Wall talks
about us being 'a distinctive in the grey'.

So why else should we bother with schools? A very
simple reason is that schools struggle. A lot of teachers and
other staff are ill with stress. We can be good news to
schools and not be a drain on them. Some Christians go
into school and make demands – they need this, they need
that, and they expect the school to run round and serve
them. We need to have an attitude of blessing teachers so
that they smile when they see us.

One of my head teachers was chatting with me and I asked her what had been the best thing about my working in her school. She said, 'It's your reliability.' I was a little bit disappointed at first. I thought, 'Oh great, so it wasn't the

---
'Dependability is one of the key things that we need to model.'
---

excellent talks we did or the way we impacted young people's lives in the small groups we led.' She said, 'It's being reliable, because we have had a lot of people come into school and promise this and that but actually they don't deliver – they don't turn up on time or they come for three weeks and never come back again. The great thing about you is we know when you are coming and you are on time.' Dependability is one of the key things that we need to model, and that in itself is a reason to bother with schools. We can bring them some stability.

I often wonder why there aren't more people involved in schools work, and as I travel around visiting different places and different churches, I think some of it is because of our teaching about spiritual gifts. One of the reasons we should bother with schools is that we as a church have a lot to offer. We have a lot of individuals with great gifts, but they are often not able to see an outlet for them. It is almost as though the only way we can serve in the church is to be a leader or be in the worship group or make the tea. If there is someone sitting in a congregation who is a football coach, or experienced in business or fund raising, let's offer those gifts to schools. One hour a week running a football club, or a couple of hours serving on a governing body, would release their creativity and gifts into the school (and other environments), which would be a blessing to our local communities.

We have loads to offer no matter how old we are or what our gifts are, and being a good communicator is not the only gift that is required to be a schools worker. Simply being a role model is an excellent reason to bother with schools. As I have grown up as a Christian I've thought about Christian role models and how Christians are portrayed in the media, and there are some great examples like Chris Akabusi and Steve Chalke. But to be honest, most people's view of Christians leaves a lot lacking – Harold of *Neighbours*, Dot Cotton from *Eastenders*, a doddery (or adulterous) old vicar and the first woman to disappear from *Big Brother*! They don't come across as having the life of Jesus in them. They say they are Christians, or they are 'religious', and it goes no further than that. Even when Nick Cotton came back to *Eastenders*, saying he was a Christian, he ended up trying to murder his mum! Young people just don't know that Christians are normal people who laugh, cry and break wind! I have had the privilege of being able to break down the big barriers with young people in school enough for them to say, 'Well, Christians are OK.'

Maybe the two biggest barriers we can break down are in establishing that 'Christians are OK' and 'God loves me'. If we can get that across to young people then they have got a much more realistic impression of a third of the world's population! That will do me for a start!

The Evangelical Alliance in their *Idea* magazine (March 2002) say that 'there are few better opportunities for Christians to be a movement for change than through education'. That quote, I believe, suggests an answer to the appalling church attendance figures we have seen bandied around over the last few years. I don't want to blind you with figures, but here are a couple of key statistics that have helped me to realise the importance of schools work.

> 41% (or two churches in every 5) in England have no young people in their congregation or Sunday school at all . . . There was also a particular drop around the Year 8 mark in young people . . . One Anglican deanery in South East England surveyed 13 churches and in Year 8 it actually peaked . . . 19% of the young people in their church were of Year 8, then by the time they got to Year 9 it had dropped to 4%. (*Quadrant*, September 2001, Christian Research)

These early years are especially key, not just for church attendance but also for shaping the independence coming upon the lives of young people. Maybe these startling figures show us how we should spend our money in a church context by concentrating on that 11 to 14 age bracket.

I found the following figure took a little bit of believing. It comes from the *Finding Faith in 1994* survey for Churches Together in England, and it says, 'It is still true that 70% of those who come to faith do so before the age of 20.' Now if that isn't a reason to bother with schools or for churches to prioritise youth work I don't know what is!

Commenting on the English church attendance survey, Dr Peter Brierley from Christian Research gives us this staggering comment on page 98 of *The Tide is Running Out*: 'Apart from a revival it is difficult to see how the church can reverse such a steep downward trend. We are one generation from extinction.' It goes on to summarise that half of the overall loss of church attendance in the 1990s was among children under the age of 15. As quoted earlier, many children today think mosaically and the church has to find better ways of relating to them. At the risk of being unpopular, I have to ask, 'Has Sunday church or Sunday School become irrelevant to children and young people in this nation?' Before you put the book down and get depressed, I want to encourage you with the amazing opportunities that the law has given us to be involved in schools.

First an extract from the 1988 Education Reform Act. This is a really important piece of legislation, which talks about a daily act of collective worship (or, as I would call it, 'assembly') in schools.

> Section 7: Special provisions as to collective worship in county schools, sub section 1. Subject to the following provisions of this section in the case of a county school the collective worship required in the school by section 6 of this Act shall be wholly or mainly of a broadly Christian character.
>
> Sub section 2: For the purposes of sub section 1 above, collective worship is of a broadly Christian character if it reflects the broad traditions of Christian belief without being distinctive of any particular Christian denomination.
>
> Sub section 3: Every act of collective worship required by section 6 of this act in the case of a county school need not comply with sub section 1 above provided that, taking any school term as a whole, most such acts which take place in the school do comply with that sub section.

My own paraphrase of that would be that all county schools are required by law, and will be inspected by OFSTED, to provide a daily act of collective worship of a mainly Christian character. We will discuss assemblies further in a later chapter; however, just at this point it is good to note that here is a great opportunity for us. Head teachers and senior staff are usually responsible for assemblies and are desperate for help because of the demands of teaching. Is it right for someone who is not a Christian to do a Christian talk? It must be the most uncomfortable thing to do, and most of my teachers are really glad to have help in any way!

There are also many aspects of RE lessons where Christians can help, especially when there is material on baptism, church and Jesus in the RE syllabus. These are great opportunities as RE is a legal requirement for all schools in England and Wales. In fact OFSTED positively encourages Christian visitors to schools as it increases the learning opportunities of young people. Alison Farnell from the Stapleford Centre has said that possibly our greatest opportunity today in schools is the whole curriculum based around citizenship, which the government is implementing as of September 2002. Each secondary school in England and Wales will have to deliver a whole scheme of work around what it means to be a citizen in today's society and all issues surrounding that. Most of this will be done through PSHE (Personal Social and Health Education) but we as Christians can offer so much in this area of citizenship and what it is to impact and contribute to society. We have already heard stories about schools workers who have planned a programme and their school has implemented it. Keep your eyes and ears open for this.

Alison goes on to explain the importance of the National Curriculum, its values, aims and purposes and the opportunities it gives to us as Christians. Aim 2 of the National Curriculum England 2000 (following on from previous 1990 and 1992 legislation) says this:

The school curriculum should aim to promote pupils' spiritual, moral, social and cultural development and prepare all pupils for the opportunities, responsibilities and experiences of life.

So schools are now obligated to develop the moral and spiritual side of children's education across the curriculum, and that means there need to be spiritual and moral aspects to Maths, English and other subjects including computer education. This is obviously another reason to bother with schools – they need our help!

Quoting directly out of the *Handbook for Secondary Teachers in England*, published in 2000:

> All national curriculum subjects provide opportunities to promote pupils' spiritual, moral, social and cultural development, explicit opportunities to promote pupils' development in these areas and provide religious education, citizenship and the non-statutory framework for personal, social and health education (PSHE) at key stages 3 and 4. A significant contribution is also made by school ethos, effective relationships throughout the school, collective worship (assemblies) and other curriculum activities.
>
> Pupils' spiritual development involves the growth of their sense of self, their unique potential, their understanding of their strengths and weaknesses and their will to achieve. As their curiosity about themselves and their place in the world increases they try to answer for themselves some of life's fundamental questions. They develop the knowledge, skills, understanding qualities and attitudes they need to foster their inner lives and non material well being.

Occasionally we can thank God for legal documents!

4

Check Your Head!

At some time in the past I must have given my telephone number to a company that has sold it to a lot of people. About once a week now I get a phone call which usually starts off something like, 'Is Mr Jackson there? This is just a courtesy call from You Need Some More Windows PLC, just wondering . . .' Some of the cleverer ones will actually speak to you for a couple of minutes without ever getting to the point, but now I can spot them a mile off and politely put the phone down on them.

It's a little bit like that in school because Christians approach schools with hidden agendas or motives – a special Christian version of tele-sales people! The school might well be taken in a couple of times but soon learns to spot people like that very quickly.

I had a bit of a rude awakening when I first started my job as a schools worker. I had chosen four schools to work in on a full-time basis. I approached this quite posh school, had a cup of tea with the head and told him about Leeds Faith In Schools and what I was able to offer. Someone else had already made an approach on my behalf so it wasn't a cold contact, but to my surprise the conversation suddenly stopped and he said to me, 'Why should I let you into my school? Why should I let you teach my children?'

'His mindset was, "If you are not a qualified teacher you shouldn't be here in my school."'

Having been in the job only a few weeks, I was taken aback by this direct question. I felt I had been naughty in class! I realised later there were several reasons why he made these comments, including the fact that he'd had a bad experience from visiting Christian groups several years ago where the only thing he remembered about them was 'they were very, very noisy'. His mindset was, 'If you are not a qualified teacher you shouldn't be here in my school.'

Looking back I'm really glad now to have had that hair-raising experience, because it made me think immediately 'Why am I here? What is the purpose of my being in the school? What are my motives?' Thankfully I'd had some help from some wise people and I managed to talk my way through it. I could honestly say to him, 'I want to be a Christian resource to your school.' Once we'd talked through what that could mean, he became more open to me and I went on to work there for a couple of years.There is still a Christian presence in that school to date.

To be honest, I know I'm an evangelist (in the Ephesians 4 capacity) but I work in a school environment, so what does that mean? The fact is I realised I did want people to become disciples of Jesus and learn more about Christianity, but I also wanted to be a help and a genuine resource, and if I didn't have that servant motive then it would have 'stuck out like a sore thumb'. It is helpful to understand why you want to be involved in schools so that you can hold your hands up and say, 'Look, this is what I'm here for.'

Pip Wilson was the developer of The Rolling Magazine tent at Greenbelt many years ago and he wrote a couple of good books as well. He talks about being a 'palm person'. If you are showing your palms to somebody, that shows openness and vulnerability. It's good to develop this attitude so that you can go in to see a head teacher or a senior member of staff, open your palms to them (metaphorically!) and say honestly, 'Look, this is what I'm about; this is where I am coming from. Can I help you?' 'You can persuade others if you are wise and speak sensibly' (Proverbs 16:23 CEV).

We need to be 'as gentle as a dove' when we are in a school situation. We don't want to always have all the answers, but we need to bring the presence and peace of God there. If I go into a school and say, 'Hi there, I'm an evangelist, can I help you?' the cultural connotations of evangelism will go before me and you know they are thinking of American TV evangelists and my asking for their money or doing 'appeals' in assemblies! I don't even mention Leeds Faith In Schools because to them it doesn't mean anything. What they understand is I'm a person who's reliable and useful.

True contextualisation is what I mean, and that doesn't involve 'hiding' or 'bending' the truth. It doesn't mean syncretism either. White supremacies have done this with Christianity, where they actually drop or add part of the true doctrine to identify with other people or make a point that is not in Scripture. Ajith Fernando describes contextualisation as inviting your Muslim neighbour for Christmas dinner and not serving pork, or not serving beef when you invite your devout Hindu for a meal. We need to be aware of cultural differences, and schools have cultural differences just as foreign mission fields do.

> The weakness that many Christians encounter today is that of frustration. While the modern emphasis on efficiency has produced quick ways to do many things, there is no shortcut to effective evangelism. This may be the single biggest challenge that Western missionaries will face in the twenty-first century. They are not skilled at facing frustration, but if they are to be effective missionaries they will have to master that skill. This skill is not necessarily only for missionaries. All Christians need it! We must persevere in loving a roommate whose salvation we desire but who just scoffs at all things Christian. We need patience to keep an unbelieving spouse open to the possibility of responding to the gospel. We must face frustration in our work place when our Christian principles are scorned and we are constantly humiliated because of them. (Ajith Fernando, *Sharing the Truth in Love*, Discovery House Publishers 2001)

The sociologist Paul Hiebert calls this 'critical contextualisation'. That is what I did with that head teacher when I contextualised my beliefs into the culture and language he understood, and that's simply what Jesus and Paul did in their day.

If you are contacting schools only for your own purposes then I can think of schools workers and staff across the country who will say 'Please don't bother!'. It's usually divisive and just not helpful. A friend of mine invited someone into his school from a church nearby: he was a very charismatic character and did an excellent set of lessons, but he was only there to invite the young people to his church and had little local knowledge or contacts. Yes, he might have done some great lessons, but actually the reason he was there was that he had a youth event on and he was wanting, in whatever way he could, to get them to go. He may have thought it a genuine reason, but hidden agendas are divisive and not godly. They also end up promoting denominationalism. One of the first things you have to learn is that being a schools worker is being a servant of the kingdom of God and not any particular church or denomination, even if you are employed by a particular church.

One of the strengths of Leeds Faith In Schools is that we have trustees and workers from right across the denominational spectrum from Brethren to Catholic and everybody in between! This shows breadth and depth, and it shows that we are not promoting one particular cause. Schools feel so strongly about non-denominationalism that it is even mentioned in the National Curriculum that 'Christians should not promote one particular denominational stream in their contact with schools'.

If I have rattled your cage in this chapter – then great! Better rattled now than in front of a stern head teacher! Ask yourself, 'What are my motives for being in schools?'

5

Mind Your Language (and Your Culture)

In the nineteenth century thousands of British missionaries went to unexplored parts of the world when imperial colonial ambitions gave them an unparalleled chance to do that. Both men and women arrived to spread the gospel and start churches, but as Steve Chalke remarks in his book *Things Jesus Never Said:*

Few of them had any real skill in discerning what was genuinely ungodly in the native traditions and cultures they encountered and what was just a different way of doing things. All too often they made no real effort to distinguish what was Christian from what was British as it was something that they never had to do in the UK; instead they simply assumed that since Britain was a Christian country, British ways were inevitably Christian ways and vice versa. Tragically the legacy of that mistake is still obvious today in a great many churches in what were once British colonies. I visited churches where congregations are all dressed in suits in sweltering temperatures where services are in English rather than the people's indigenous language and where the music seems to have undergone a rhythm bypass operation. Many have hardly changed their format since the day the missionaries left. More than anything else they are a dull echo of old-fashioned Victorian society half a world away and 100 years on.

No matter how exciting or outward-looking we think our churches are, we still have this bizarre culture which is attached to the things that we do. Some of it, interestingly enough, is never actually taught but is just implied.

Is there such a thing as 'culture-free Christianity'?

It has been said that Christians ask people to follow a madman and join the most boring people in the world! Someone once described being in a church as similar to being on a bus – you all sit in rows facing the front, there is a driver at the front, you talk occasionally but not very often and, for those of you that are old enough to remember, halfway through someone comes round and collects your money. I find it fascinating to see the culture that we as Christians have found ourselves in.

Is there such a thing as 'culture-free Christianity'? As a youth worker and schools worker I have become more and more aware that my culture rubs off onto the young people that I work with. Anyone who is a significant role model to young people will know that the young people become like them in some way. A scary thought! This is especially true if a young person comes to faith and you have a discipling role in their life. Even the way you pray will rub off on them!

It is vitally important that we know where the line is drawn between what is Christian and what is cultural. Young people understand very little about Christianity and even less about the language that we take for granted in a church situation. The classic example of this is the word 'sin'. A tiny little word – I know what it means, you probably know what it means and most people over the age of 40 probably know what it means. Generation X didn't really understand it, so Generation Y certainly won't get it! It just doesn't mean anything to them, not because they can't read a dictionary, but because it comes with the connotations that the media have portrayed of Christianity and the overuse or misuse of the word.

Bill Hogg, a guy who worked for YFC (Youth for Christ) in Scotland, used to tell the story about how he went to the SIN–E–MA because the church wouldn't allow him to go to the cinema. (You have to shout it in a Scottish accent to get the full effect!) Young people might see stereotypical, red-faced preachers shouting 'There's sin in your lives', but they don't really know what it means because they have just shut themselves off to that word. In Leeds city centre there is often a group of aggressive preachers that shout and scream at passers-by – they have been put in prison for it in the past. One day I saw a woman preaching, and a group of lads were winding her up and throwing things at her. She ignored them and carried on shouting. I did feel sorry for her but she just didn't get it – the way she was speaking and the words she used did not connect with anyone, especially the young people around her. I tried to talk to one of these preachers once, but I seemed to be speaking a different language, which I suppose wasn't too far from the truth.

I very rarely use the word 'sin' in a school situation; I usually say something like 'the things that we do wrong' or 'the things that hurt God'. Sin is our rebellion against God. It is important for them to understand what it means, but they won't unless we explain it to them. The best talk in the world can be completely ruined by a young person not understanding one word at the beginning. 'Today I am going to talk about sin!' SLAM! The doors close, the shutters go down and they are thinking about text messaging immediately. It's the equivalent of having your flies undone in an assembly – you can talk but don't expect them to listen!

There are loads of words you can think of similar to sin in our mad Christian language. If you work in an outreach team or belong to a housegroup or cell, it's fun to brainstorm as many religious words or phrases as you can and vow not to use them. In a church situation it is not helpful to use them, and even less so in the so-called 'big bad world'.

I believe the Bible is the inspired word of God, but sometimes people need help in understanding the terminology. The New International Version of the Bible is a popular version, but it contains words that I hardly understand myself, like iniquities and transgressions. I never use these words in my normal speech, so why should I when I am talking with God? Isn't it simpler to use the normal language in which we talk to our friends or dad?

As for which versions of the Bible to use in a school situation, I use a selection. *The Message* is often very helpful, although it is slightly American. (John Buckeridge called it the Gospel according to John Wayne!) The Youth Bible is the New Century Version with some youth bits added to it. It isn't specifically in youth language, but it is quite a good version. *The Good News Bible* is also pretty simple to read for young people. I usually look at three or four different versions of the Bible (even kiddies' versions) some of which you can get on CD-ROM now, which makes it a little easier when preparing something like a Powerpoint presentation,

OHPs, or just for reading aloud in the classroom situation. Some Bible scholars will probably go mad when I say that in a totally non-Christian environment it is often better to make your own paraphrase of the Bible for certain verses. It is also vital to remember that it doesn't mean anything to young people if you say, 'This is from the first book of Corinthians,' because they think Corinthians is a Greek holiday travel brochure. So I often say, 'This is from the second part of the Bible, called the New Testament, and from a letter a guy called Paul wrote to the Christians in Corinth.' Little things like that can take away some of the mystery of the 'spooky Bible' and make it a whole lot more accessible.

A lot of churches appear to be catching 'a culture of openness'; let's not be afraid to challenge each other about the words we use and the phrases that have become commonplace in our language and almost ingrained into our Christian culture. They mean little to us but, more importantly, nothing to people outside the church.

Another problem I have found with young lads in particular is that Christian worship can appear to be quite feminine sometimes. The songs we sing and the things we say, such as 'God, you're lovely, God, you're precious' can be a real put off and a million miles from where they are at, living on a diet of Bravo, Playstation 2 and FHM.

We were having a Rock Solid group in school one lunchtime and a group of lads were hanging about outside the door, slamming the door and running off down the corridor. I can handle that, you get used to it after a while, but as it went on throughout the session it eventually interrupted what we were doing and became a real distraction. I went out of the door to see who was responsible for it, but of course there was no one there and 'no one knew anything about it'. So I waited until it happened again: the door opened, something rude was shouted into the room, the door slammed and then I heard this flurry of footsteps running up the corridor. I opened the door and sprinted as fast as I could up the corridor, and eventually caught up with the lad responsible. To see the expression on his face was a picture because (a) he didn't think I could run that fast and (b) he never expected a Christian to stand up for himself. I promptly escorted him to the head's office and was met by the 'scary' deputy head who said, 'No problem, Lee, I'll deal with him.' He was disciplined appropriately for messing up Rock Solid.

That is not the sort of thing I would do when I first come into school, but as I had known the school for a long time, I decided that those lads in Year 11 needed to understand something about Christians. I likened it to Jesus turning the tables over in the temple – sometimes you have just got to show young people that what we believe and what we are doing in school is important. I'm sure that lad had more respect for Christianity after that incident. The non-Christian deputy head also felt the same way, and it brought me a feeling of being valued in school, which kept me going.

I'm the first to admit that I'm not immune to culture and language differences, as most of my friends will tell you, but I've really made an effort to make things understandable, because only then are we able to give people the opportunities to respond and to dig deeper into God. The golden rule to remember is people do not always hear exactly what you say!

Sort it out!

1. Brainstorm the Christian and over-politically correct phrases and words you use regularly, which you would want to avoid when talking to young people.
2. Give someone permission to comment on your speech and how it appears to them.

6

First Approaches

If you've got this far, I obviously haven't put you off! The following is a guide, not a guaranteed formula.

Research

Before approaching a school, do a bit of research on two levels. First, make sure you know your area, know your school and know the catchment area. What kind of young people are in that school, what kinds of background are they from, what's the ethnic mix and what is the religious representation? That's quite easy to find out just by asking parents and people that you know who go to the school, and the information may even be available on the council websites if you check it out.

Second, find out who is working there already. You need to look for Christian staff (I deliberately use the word staff and not just teachers, as there are lots of support staff now, from office staff to technicians). It is so important to use your contacts to research what is going on in the school. I think it is asking for trouble if you approach a school without finding out more about it. There is a school that I deliberately don't go into because there are loads of Christians already involved and actually another school needed my help a lot more than that one. But I wouldn't have known that if I hadn't done the research, asked around, rang up pastors, youth leaders and anyone else around the place. While you are doing that you need to be praying to God to help your research, asking him not only to bless what you do but whether you should do it in the first place.

Start to connect with the school; maybe go to the school grounds and pray around the school, when lessons are not on. We have done some prayer walks quietly round schools and been amazed at the things that God has spoken to us about. Connecting with somewhere and being identified with that place is a way of 'softening the ground'. It is also important not to treat it lightly – you can go straight into a school but it is good to have some prayer support behind you. Tell some people what you are doing and encourage them to pray for you as you make the approaches. If you do find out that there are people in the schools who are Christians, meet them quietly and pray for them, or with them, before making any official kind of approach, and respect them and honour them for the work that they have put in for years.

Two friends of mine who are teachers in a Leeds school said that for years they used to go round the school building praying. That was before any outside Christians had any impact in the school. Now that school has a great Christian team working there which is very much part of the fabric of the school. I wonder whether that would have happened if these faithful people hadn't spent time praying. As you pray you will probably also get a sense of God's calling. Are you called to primary or secondary, or age groups within that? Who do you work best with? Is it the smaller children, the wide-eyed primary assemblies that you get with reception classes, or is it the sulky sixth formers who need impressing?

If you are a church leader or a youth worker then contact the young people that you know and ask them about their school and what is happening in there. Be prepared for an honest answer!

The approach

The best way is to write to the school and ask them respectfully if you can support them. Tell them about your gifts and abilities and give them a reference or the name of someone they can contact. It is probably best to follow this with a phone call and informal visits to the school, maybe get a guided tour round the school, learn some of the teachers' names, and get the prospectus from reception. Make sure you get to know the staff and then you can be a blessing to the school. If they have visitors' badges make sure you wear one and put your first name on it so that people can see your name quickly.

'I knew a staff room that felt like a western saloon!'

Maybe go into the staff room for a coffee. Staff rooms are difficult places – be aware that people like their own seats and have their own cups and their own coffee. If in doubt, ask, and I'm sure someone will be able to help you. I knew a staff room that felt like a western saloon! Whenever someone who wasn't a teacher used to walk in, you could hear the door close behind them and the tumbleweed drifting across the floor. Even the piano player stopped playing!

It was a very scary experience, yet I have been quite happy to be in other staff rooms, where people shout across the room and say hello to you. So don't be intimidated! It is a good place to be just to get your face known around the school. It is important to smile and say hello to nearly everyone you meet in the corridor. It really makes a difference.

Here are some tips:

- A police (CRB) check is compulsory for all who might come into contact with children.
- As you continue with the first approaches, remember that your schools work starts as you leave your house. It starts with the way you drive, the speed you drive at, driving into school at certain times and being very careful not to offend people or park in the head teacher's parking space (as I have done!).
- Once you are part of the school environment (especially if you are in a secondary school) there could be 1500 pupils who suddenly know you. So when you are in Sainsbury's or Netto's doing your shopping, be aware that if you are having an argument with your husband or your wife then there might be loads of kids around watching you do it! I tell my workers that we are 'public property' although that is not strictly true. We are on show though; and for some people that is a real problem, but I actually find it quite enjoyable. Even when I had two months off work recently, I was still seeing kids from the school that I work in and of course I can't ignore them just because I'm off work!
- Be careful of school politics – don't be seen as being in one camp or another but remain an unbiased listener.
- Don't close a door. Far too many Christians in the past have actually closed doors, which have been hard to

open again in schools. We are there to open doors, or to put our foot in the door to keep doors open. Make sure that even if an approach to a school doesn't work out, you are the one who has helped the door to remain open and not slam behind you.

Above all other things in your approach to school, and the early days in school, be reliable. Turn up before you will say you'll turn up, make sure you don't have to rush off afterwards, and just be a faithful person. Come prepared, get your equipment ready if you need it, and be as self-sufficient and reliable as you can.

Think ahead even at an early stage, because you'll be surprised at how the pace can pick up in school. A friend of mine who is the head of PE at a school in Leeds talked to me about lunchtime clubs and Rock Solid. By the next week, he'd got a room and they'd started the club!

Think about what you can offer them:

- What will happen at Christmas time?
- Will they have a special Easter celebration?
- What happens at the end of term – will there be presentations?
- Remember things like exam times and training days.

The Quality/Quantity diagram on the next page is something I find helpful to think about when we approach different levels of contacts with young people in a school environment.

- What are you doing now and what part of the triangle is it in?
- How effective is it?

- Does it fit with your goals?
- Do you need to go deeper?

Quantity

Assembly
Lesson
Group team
'Hanging out'
One to one

Quality

Finally, like all good Scouts and Guides – be prepared!
Think of all the questions you could be asked by the school
and have a good answer for them.

7

Planning Assemblies, Lessons and Clubs

We all have different personality types and ways of working, but hopefully some of the tips here will avoid that awful feeling of 'I've got a lesson in an hour's time and I don't know what to do'.

Diary it

The first thing I have found the most helpful is to use my diary correctly and to think ahead. If you have been booked for something in school which is maybe a week or even a few weeks away, then keep a running list of ideas, quotes and things to use so that when you come up with an idea you are able to write it down immediately before it is lost in a busy day. This not only helps life to be less stressful with fewer ideas bouncing around in your head, but it is also more effective.

Map it

I like to use something called mindmapping or spider-grams. It's a way of encouraging creativity without 'linear' thinking. Lists stifle my creativity. I have found using blank pieces of paper really worked for me. I went to the local art shop and got a hardback sketch book which had perforated pages so that I could tear them out. I carry this book pretty much everywhere I go. Even though I use a palm organiser (PDA) for sorting out my diary and everything else, I still find it difficult to plan on a computer device, so I always have this book around with me to keep things going. The strength of planning like this is that you don't put anything in any order. Ideas, no matter how wacky and strange, can be put down on a piece of paper and can then be prioritised or crossed out at a later stage.

I may actually write the talk on a piece of card to prompt me, or do it on the computer on an A4 sheet, but only after the mindmap stage. Often I just take the map with me and do the lesson from that.

Here is an example of how I would use a mindmap to plan a PSE lesson . . .

I start with this . . .

PSE lesson
Y9 – Confidence
26/2/02
(lesson 5 of 6)

add things as I think of them . . .

trust games?

bullying scenario?

group questions
how can we be more confident?
is confidence being loud or calm?

A personal story

PSE lesson

Icebreaker game ——— **Y9 – Confidence**
26/2/02
(lesson 5 of 6)

Video clips*
  bungee jump world record
  The Fugitive jump into dam

Feedback from last week

*Video follow-up questions:
    What was the difference in the jumps?
    (one guy knew he would survive, the
    other didn't)
    What does that teach us?

and finally put them in some sort of order!

1. Feedback from last week
2. Icebreaker game
3. Video clips
4. Video follow-up questions:
   What was the difference in the jumps?
   What does that teach us?
5. Group questions:
   How can we be more confident?
   Is confidence being loud or calm?
6. A personal story

Extra: Trust games; bullying scenario.

I never write the talk out in full; I prefer to use bullet points to remind me what to say or to keep me on track. The main problem I have in school is not necessarily what to say, but what not to say. If you have five minutes to do a presentation it is very easy to talk about life, the world, the universe, the whole gospel and everything else, but the bell will have gone before you have made the point you were trying to make! You may also find it useful to go on a Myers Briggs or similar personality testing course to find out more about your brain and how it works.

Give yourself time to think about talks and use the things around you in the world. As I am driving around the city from school to school I might be listening to the radio and hear a particular song which would fit in with a talk, or I may hear details of a new film which has come out. Use something from the culture which points towards what God is going to say through you. It helps to hook people first to keep their attention longer.

Is there a video clip you can use? You need to watch them several times, looking for suitable slots of between two and five minutes. Give a good explanation beforehand. If it's a film you know well, remember the young people might not know it, so make sure you explain what it is about. It is very rarely you get a video clip which actually finishes a point for you, so use it as a springboard to make a point or move on to the next section of the talk.

Audio clips can also be used, or even just chill-out music. If I am doing group work, it is often good to have something in the background which breaks the silence and may also speak into the subject without people even knowing it. For example, when doing a lesson on 'Who is Jesus?' with Year 8 RE, we went into the ten-minute group discussion time and put on the song 'One of Us' by

Joan Osborne as we talked about 'What if God was one of us?'

Here are some more tips:

- If you are not experienced, plan half as much again as you will need; this will just help you pull things together if the young people don't talk to you and it goes a lot quicker than you expect!
- In a lesson situation I like to keep things fairly flexible. It is important to have a good beginning and a good end to any presentation, but some of the bits in the middle can be left without spoiling the point you are addressing.
- Steal it but own it! Schools workers, like all good Christian communicators, steal most of their material because, after all, who has ever had an original idea? Make sure it has not been used in that school before, and also own it, because it means nothing to anyone if it is not personal to you.
- Research what you are doing. Make sure you know what the year group is, what level they are on, whether it is a streamed class or a mixed-ability class, with bright kids or the kids that struggle a bit more, and whether there are any special needs children in the lesson. Don't forget your jargon buster.
- Don't ever talk about something you are not sure about. Don't be afraid to say no if you have been asked to do a sixth form lesson on eschatology, for example, – it's not 'the end of the world' to admit it's not your field. Always talk about what you know, and if you don't know then go away and find out about it for later.
- Does the teacher expect you to use handouts, or do they

expect you to set homework? I have only set homework a couple of times in my work in school but it was relevant for that situation.

- In an assembly have one point to get across. In lessons the same still applies but obviously you can approach it from different angles, so try and make your conclusion a good one.

- Understand the strengths and weaknesses of the people you are working with. If you are taking someone in with you who is very quiet, they will be the best person to pray or help with small group work, and you will be the person to do the up-front stuff. However, if there is someone there who is very confident and outgoing then share those opportunities with them and allow the strengths and weaknesses of the team to come out. Maybe put the names of people next to job roles as you start pulling the team together.

- Chat with God about the things you would like to speak about, and you will soon find that ideas come to your mind. Ask people's advice on subjects you are talking about. Get a big piece of paper out and brainstorm a lesson, and before you know it you'll have most of your lesson ready because everyone has chipped in with their ideas. I really believe that people with small pieces of paper will have small ideas, so don't be afraid to get big pieces of paper and marker pens.

- Get out in the open, walk around, think and pray and write things down rather than being hunched over a desk with a little piece of A5 paper and a badly sharpened pencil. Be creative, step out and think big.

Pulling a programme together

- Make sure everyone is there as you look at the diary. We don't start in the first week of term as it is often a little bit mad in school. Allow a week's grace and go in on the second week of term.
- Have a planning meeting. It doesn't have to be for very long but get people together and plan ahead. It is best to do it together and you will find that the ideas and the creativity will come.
- Allow your programme to be flexible. If you are doing a programme of lessons or clubs, things may change – you may have been asked to do six lessons, one per week, but be aware that one lesson might go very well and you might want to continue that subject the week after. So don't set it in stone. So far as groups are concerned allow a bit of space for questions, or for a visitor once or twice a term. Sometimes just have a party and celebrate events, such as Christmas, Easter and the end of year!
- Be aware of school training days. They are usually written down in the calendar. If not, get to know the receptionist well and make sure they will ring you if they know. There is not much point doing schools work if there are no kids in the building!

8

How to Deliver a Good Assembly

Ninety per cent of the assemblies I do will include some sort of game which will require volunteers. The reason I do that is not because the game is significant, although often the games are related to the subject, however loosely. But if you get young people or their friends helping out with a game, they get a little bit of stardom that will hold their attention for the few minutes afterwards when you deliver a short talk.

I believe most schools work should be based around chocolate! Not only was cocoa created by the Lord himself, but it is a great incentive. So if you get volunteers in assembly make sure they have a prize of some chocolate, or something more expensive if you are feeling flush. Even if it is a competition and somebody wins, make sure that all of the volunteers get a prize as well. It is important to value them not as winners and losers but as people. How you treat volunteers and people in assemblies is just as important as the things that you say.

I was taking an assembly in front of 600 pupils, the whole of key stage 3 (Years 7–9), and I asked for two volunteers for a quiz. All the hands shot up as usual from the younger pupils and I chose a girl and a boy. Because they were a fairly new year group I didn't know them very well, and as I chose the boy and he stood up I suddenly noticed that all the teachers started talking to each other and there was a lot of mumbling. As he got to the front it was apparent the lad I had chosen had particular special needs. All the teachers and pupils were watching me very carefully to see how I dealt with him. Because it was a quiz I did go through it with him very carefully, but he wasn't able to answer any questions and the girl won. It was so important that I honour this lad, who had had the guts to put his hand up and come out in front of all the people in his year, so I made sure he got a prize and a big round of applause afterwards.

- Choose volunteers carefully. If you get no hands going up then ask one of the teachers to choose for you, and that will remove any embarrassment and any of the concerns you may have over the volunteers. I must admit I tend to live a little bit more by the seat of my pants and like to see what will happen.
- Get people to give a round of applause as the volunteers come out to the front and make sure they get a round of applause at the end, so they go out feeling really good about themselves
- Be aware that if you do decide to do a game in assembly, not all games that you do in youth groups are appropriate for schools. Large banana splits, egg-related games and other mad things are not appropriate for school mainly because of the mess and the nightmare you have afterwards cleaning it up.
- If I have got a lot of equipment to set up I often ask the kids to help me. They usually like to be involved,

and helping to press 'play' on the CD player, for example, means they get to sit on a chair instead of on the floor!

The time before and after assemblies is just as important as the assemblies themselves, so be aware of the way you treat people as you set up and pack things away.

Instead of talking about a concept from your faith, it is much better to make it personal and talk about your life, your job, your dog, the sports that you play, TV that you watch, and the things that happen in your family life. I was doing an assembly once and decided to add an illustration I hadn't planned on. I started talking about my dating Clare before we were married. I looked across the assembly hall and realised all eyes were transfixed on me! I discovered the power of personal testimony that day. There is a danger, of course, that you could share too much, so be careful, but it is much more interesting to young people than 'the Bible says'.

Using the Bible in an assembly is notoriously difficult. Sometimes I will read something, and then tell them it is from the Bible, because if I tell them *beforehand* I can often hear groans (especially in secondary schools). Don't hide the Bible from them but find creative ways to use it.

Everyone has their own style, but following is a general pattern that I work to when doing assemblies. (Remember in secondary schools you will get 5 to 10 minutes and 10 to 25 minutes in primary school.)

1. Intro myself (and team)
2. Game (and video clip if time allows)
3. Short talk
4. One-line conclusion

Expect the unexpected and be flexible. I make sure I plan a ten-minute assembly for a secondary school, but I have sometimes been given just two or three minutes so something has to go! Please see Appendix 3 for three sample assembly outlines.

9

RE and PSHE

Schools workers across the country have been involved in all kinds of lessons in school, from design and technology to music and even maths lessons! However, most opportunities for Christians in lessons will come in two areas: either RE (Religious Education) or PSHE (Personal Social and Health Education). Sarah Bradford and I will deal with those two in this chapter.

Religious Education

RE is compulsory and yet not part of the National Curriculum; another one of those strange anomalies, which happen with school curriculum policies. For those interested, this is explored fully in Janet King's book *Teaching RE in Secondary Schools*, published by ACT and Monarch.

Let us see what the government says about this. The following is taken from the *National Curriculum 2000 Handbook for Secondary Teachers in England* and it is available on www.nc.uk.net.

Under the Education Act 1996 schools must provide religious education for all registered pupils, although parents can choose to withdraw their children. Schools, other than voluntary aided schools and those of a religious character, must teach religious education according to the locally agreed syllabus. Each agreed syllabus should reflect the fact that the religious traditions in Great Britain are in the main Christian, while taking account of the teachings and practices of the other principal religions represented in Great Britain.

Religious education makes a distinctive contribution to the school curriculum by developing pupils' knowledge and understanding of religion, religious beliefs, practices, language and traditions and their influence on individuals, communities, societies and cultures. It enables pupils to consider and respond to a range of important questions related to their own spiritual development, the development of values and attitudes and fundamental questions concerning the meaning and purpose of life.

We have a lot to offer to RE departments in school at both primary and secondary level. However, it is important to understand the context in which RE is taught in this country. The Leeds agreed syllabus for Religious Education published in 1996 is fairly typical of other Education Authorities in England. The foreword says this:

> The Leeds LEA has long held that Religious Education must not be confused with instruction. It is achieved through teaching not preaching; by being neither narrow nor sectarian it aims to create citizens who can appreciate other people's beliefs as well as their own, such citizens will act with tolerance and understanding for others however different from themselves.

RE departments' primary body of study is Christianity. However, you have to understand that this is 'comparative' religion and all major faiths are also dealt with as published in your local area's agreed syllabus.

In my approach to school I found it quite difficult initially to offer myself to RE as I didn't understand fully what it entailed. The easiest way to combat this was to obtain a copy of the agreed syllabus. Once I had done that, I photocopied the syllabus and then went through with a marking pen, marking the aspects of the syllabus I felt I had knowledge of or could help with as a local Christian. This became really helpful to the RE teachers, and they would ring me up when a certain section of a syllabus was due to be taught. It can appear boring, but getting your head round it for a couple of hours and understanding about RE and the syllabus will help you with your relationships with the RE teacher and allow you to understand the big picture and the input that you can have into that.

It is not possible to show you a draft of an agreed syllabus here, but if you ask your local school they will have one in the department that they can probably give or lend to you and it may also be available from your Local Education Authority.

If you make an approach to school particularly for lessons, write a covering letter with the bits of the agreed syllabus highlighted attached to the letter and then follow it up with a visit as per normal. I found the teachers were very happy for me to be involved and it showed that I spoke the same language as them!

So what structure does a lesson have? Lessons range from 35 minutes to over an hour. The first questions to ask are always 'How long is it, what time does it start and what year groups is it with?' Once you have established those things you can use your skills to put together a lesson plan. Typically a lesson that I would deliver would consist of an introduction, a couple of short talks, maybe a work sheet or an open discussion, a video clip and anything else that would be relevant to the subject. Refer to Chapter 7 for more details and ideas. Below is a framework for you to work on. The most important thing to remember is that you cannot talk for over an hour! It is important to do exercises, games and other things that keep the young people's interest in the subject.

'There are no excuses for boring RE lessons.'

There are no excuses for boring RE lessons. You are a visitor to the school and have more opportunity to make it a fun, interactive and memorable lesson than a teacher who is there every single week. Remember that young people respond well to different things and a fresh face is helpful both to the teachers and the pupils.

Not everyone is able to deliver lessons. If you are in any doubt about what to do then try to spend some time with another schools worker who you may be able to contact via the Schools Ministry Network, or if you have a good relationship with the school, ask if you can sit in the lessons and see the kinds of thing that go on.

A draft lesson structure:

What is the Bible? Year 8, mixed ability

- Intro – using different versions of the Bible, etc.
- Physical quiz (moving around) – A, B, C around the room, pupils have to move to answer of choice.
- Info sheet on what the Bible is made up of. Get them to read it out and explain it.
- Short talk on how the Bible can be relevant today.

- Split into four groups and give each group one object to describe: lamp, milk, sword, seed. Discuss how the Bible might be described as an object.
- Feedback; then give relevant Bible verses and explain (1) lamp – Psalm 119:105; (2) milk – 1 Peter 2:2; (3) sword – Ephesians 6:17; (4) seed – Matthew 13:1–9 and 18 23.
- Look at the parable of the sower. God's word is always the same; it is how people receive it that has the main effect. Show pictures of soil type on the board and brainstorm ideas of types of people.
- Open question time or Bible bingo.

But why do RE lessons?

Abi Monteith came up with the following thoughts:

- Planting a seed that's never been there before – breaking through the ground.
- Watering a seed – bringing new life to a seed that is lying dormant.
- Fertilising the seed – bringing health and life to a seed that's already growing.
- Light – revitalising a shoot that may be diminishing.

PSHE (sometimes called PSE)

PSHE is not statutory for schools to deliver, but guidelines are produced and OFSTED do inspect it. Sarah Bradford shares some of her experience:

'We have had some great opportunities in school during the past few months through being able to offer PSHE

(Personal Social and Health Education) to the schools we work in.

'PSHE affects all other aspects of school life and as Christian youth workers it's good to have as much influence in it as possible. It is such an important part of the young people's development and learning – you can have a massive impact on the young people's morals and values. It is important to get some training; if you can offer a relevant subject, schools usually bite your hand off! We were trained by ACET (Aids Care Education and Training); they helped us to communicate all aspects of HIV and sex-related education. Find out more at www.acetuk.org. The best person to link with is the head of PSHE who is usually more than willing to have some extra help as it seems like a subject that teachers will opt out of if given the chance.

'I got into one school by connecting with the community/school nurse who belonged to one of the local churches. I went in with her and together we delivered a term of PSHE to Year 11 (eight 35-minute sessions). The pupils commented that it was really good having a nurse and also someone more their age that they could talk to. It's a good idea to have a male and female to go into the lessons if possible as there might be boy/girl issues. Because it's quite an intimate and personal subject, it seems easy to bond and connect with the young people, more so than in other lessons.

'Lessons that have worked well have been AIDS/HIV, decision-making in relationships, self-esteem, body image and contraception. The more interactive and fun the better – they love games, practical learning and group discussions more than someone just talking at them from the front. It's especially important to let them have as much of a say as possible. You are there to help them work out and develop

their own thinking. *Question and answer times have always worked well, but in some subjects the young people have wanted to be anonymous in asking their questions by writing them down.*

'You will have to be prepared for them asking you quite personal and sometimes embarrassing questions. Try not to go red and try to keep a straight face if you can! You need to learn the appropriate times of when to laugh and when not to laugh. Within a class there is such a variety of maturity levels, so be prepared! I find it exciting as a Christian to do lessons that are not directly Christian but allow us to teach that Christianity affects all aspects of our life – including our sex life!'

Top tip for lessons

If you ask the young people to ask you questions at the end of the lesson and they become silent, put them into groups of two and three to discuss the subject and come up with a question between them. This works 99 per cent of the time and has saved my life on more than one occasion!

10
Sport

At my first schools workers conference in Birmingham I heard a head teacher say in his talk that schools workers 'should get out of the classroom and into the sports hall'. It took me by surprise and, to be honest, I felt 'he's putting down my assemblies!' But that one-liner changed the way I looked at school from then on because I realised that I had missed a huge part of school life. I love basketball, in particular, but it had never crossed my mind to use it in school.

Even now youth and schools workers often do not see sport as a valid ministry option. But if we neglect the physical aspect of young people, we are not seeing them as a whole, and I can honestly say that doing basketball and sport in school has been the best ice-breaker and relationship-building tool I have used. There is something about playing sport with young people that levels the playing field (if you can excuse the pun!). The barriers are broken down when you are being tackled by 23 Year 7s.

The teachers' strike in the eighties almost destroyed sport in schools. Teachers dropped many extra curricular activities and never picked them up again afterwards. And, with the current demands on teachers, many quite rightly do not want to. There is a great need for help with all sorts of teams in school. At Allerton High, a school that I have worked in for several years, I have become the school's basketball coach, not because I am the best, but because the PE staff have a dozen other teams to run without basketball.

I started playing basketball with the sixth formers and caught the bug. The school let me start coaching without qualifications at first, but I soon took the Level 1 coaching certificate, and a couple of years later the Level 2 coaching award, which means I can coach anyone up to professional level. I told the PE staff I was doing this and that worked well because it showed that I was serious and wanted to be the best that I could be. There are a lot of awards at different levels which you can take, including general community coaching awards, which will teach you new skills, educate you about insurance and safety and help bring more professionalism to your work. Once you are qualified there may even be some funding available to pay you for community and school sessions. Contact your local council or university to see what courses are available.

Recently I was part of the process in getting one of my schools Sportsmark status, which cannot be done without schools showing community involvement in their sports programme. I am a regular member of their sports staff, yet still represent the local community, so that went in their favour on the application form. Church and school working together in this instance actually went in their favour and increased funding for the school.

If you are not sporty there is now quite a selection of Christian sports teams that you could invite into school to help you. There are Fly and Kick teams from Youth For

Christ, and also Christians in Sport and Ambassadors In
Sport: all can advise you on working with sports teams in
school. In the resources section of this book you can find
more information and contact details. Are there local professional Christian sportsmen and women in your area that
you could persuade to come into school? Use your contacts
and see what's available.

If you can also pass a minibus driver's test (PSV licence),
it helps to take teams away on your own when teachers are
not available. You cannot drive the school minibus unless
you have passed the 'blue badge' test that is reapplied for
every year.

Sport is especially a key to reaching lads in school and,
if research is anything to go by, they need people to talk to
on their level. According to the Leading Lads report
(www.topman.co.uk) only 38 per cent of lads would talk
to someone if they're worried or upset and 57 per cent of
them often feel overwhelmed by worry about schoolwork.
Sport is part of the whole package we could offer to schools
and it is a way for us to model a balanced life. Do not
dismiss it as 'not proper youth work'.

Meeting 'Carl'

I was continuing to do key stage 4 basketball training in
one of my schools on a weekly basis, as well as just hanging
around a bit in school at lunchtime playing basketball so
the kids would know me. I met Carl as he came along to
practice. He was always a little different but he became
quite a good basketball player and could certainly hold his
own with anyone in the school. Occasionally he would take
the huff and just not want to get involved in the whole
practice.

I got to know Carl pretty well through basketball and I used to spend some time talking to him after practice. This is a time not to be wasted, as often when you've relaxed and played sport with each other, young people are wanting to talk about issues that are important in their lives. Carl started telling me about his mum and dad and his family: the stresses and strains of the family relationships. Materially he seemed to have everything he wanted; all the usual trappings of computers and nice trainers. But he just wasn't happy, it was as simple as that, and during his time at basketball he became closer and closer to me and continued to chat through things.

He made a few mistakes at school and decided to just stop attending. I was in the privileged position of probably being the person in the school who knew him best, and so his year head asked me to visit him at home. It was a real privilege to see him outside the school environment with his family, and try to help him understand some of the big issues around non-attendance at school.

Sadly, after I had seen him a few times and he continued to stay off school, our relationship dried up. I didn't hear much from him so I wrote him a letter saying that I wished him all the best for his future and would continue to pray for him and ask God's blessing on his life.

He never responded to the letter, until one night after basketball practice with my team I pulled into the garage near where I live at about 9.30 pm to fill up with petrol. I heard this lad shouting to me, and across the forecourt came Carl. I was pleased to see him, even though it was my only night off. He talked to me about how he had moved into his new school and he wondered if, though he was in a different school, he would still be able to see me in a kind of mentoring capacity. He said he really appreciated the letter that I had sent him.

So my relationship with Carl is ongoing and who knows where it will end. With me not being an authority figure in his life he felt able to talk through some of the big stuff, and I count it a privilege to be part of his life, especially as it was playing sport with him that broke the ice and helped us to get to know each other.

I look forward in years to come to other stories like Carl's and more success in genuine relationships that have been built through sport.

11

Prayer – the Lost Strategy?

Schools work can easily become task-orientated, as you continually have lessons, assemblies and clubs. In your diary things seem to come round very quickly, and in all the planning and preparation often prayer can take a back seat. We can plan really well and then just say a quick prayer as we walk into school!

'Transformation is not a trick performed by God, but it is a cause and effect process.'

We recently spent a month in prayer for the youth of Leeds. Every Monday morning we had a small team of local prayers come in, then we drove to our schools, prayed round them and asked God for it to be 'fertile ground'. In his book *Informed Intercession*, George Otis Jnr (famous for the *Transformation* videos which show documentary evidence of communities that have been transformed by God) says that in 100 per cent of the cases of community transformation he studied there are two factors which are always present. One is persevering leadership and the second is fervent, informed, united and sustained prayer.

He goes on to say that transformation is not a trick performed by God, but it is a cause and effect process. It is not a feeling, it is a fact, and the question is how do we get there?

Here are a few ideas that may encourage creative prayer to be fully part of what we do in school. One of the key phrases George Otis Jnr uses is *informed* prayer, because, if you are anything like me, after a couple of minutes of praying I run out of things to say. Informed prayer for schools is very important. How can we fuel the fire of prayer?

- A church in Leeds invited members of their local community including teachers, policemen and councillors to come to the church one morning. They shared their concerns and they prayed for them.

- Have you considered writing to a head teacher, or a senior member of staff, asking them for things to pray for? You will be surprised – even if they don't believe, they will still be up for a bit of free prayer!

- Can you get a copy of the names of the pupils and teachers from the school? You could probably do this without getting addresses, which would be OK. Could you pray through those names on a regular basis?

- Do any young people or staff pray in the school at the moment? If they do, can you join them? Can you encourage them to do it if they are not?

- If there is a Christian group in the school, maybe you could encourage the idea that every other meeting is a prayer meeting. Encourage them to write to their head teacher and empower them to be a witness and an intercessor for their school.

The Bible tells us to pray for those in authority . . .

> I urge you, first of all, to pray for all people. As you make your requests, plead for God's mercy upon them, and give thanks. Pray this way for kings and all others who are in authority, so that we can live in peace and quietness, in godliness and dignity. This is good and pleases God our Savior, for he wants everyone to be saved and to understand the truth. (1 Timothy 2:1–4 NLT)

Make sure that you and your supporters are praying for Charles Clarke (or whoever the current Education Secretary may be). The Standing Advisory Council on Religious Education, the Local Education Authority, OFSTED, the head teachers, the governors and senior staff all need prayer. If we can ask God to give wisdom to these people in authority, it will make such a difference. Pray too for the teachers' unions, as they hold so much influence over things such as extra curricula activities.

Establish a prayer letter for school, but you need to be a little bit careful what you put in the prayer letter (maybe change the names of people). Why not prayer walk the school? Prayer-walking is simply identifying with the school by being there. I have prayed around a school's perimeter, I have prayed in the school grounds, I have prayed quietly (with my eyes open!) around the schools as I have walked. Taking a team of people with you helps you to focus and to reflect on what God has said as you pray.

There are all sorts of creative ways to pray. Instead of spending all of our time brainstorming lessons and assemblies, we allow different styles of prayer – quiet, loud, reflective, liturgical – to flow as we meet together to plan.

Check out www.24–7prayer.com for creative prayer ideas and maybe set up a 24–7 prayer room in a school. Or if you are doing one in church, have a section for the school where you can write the names of staff, pupils, and the things that God is doing in the school on the wall and encourage people to pray for them.

If we can get rid of our English reserve and our embarrassment of actually praying, I am sure that our schools and youth work will be much more effective in the future. I believe God has promised exciting things for his nation, so let us pray them in.

Are there some people in the church who are available during the day to pray for you as you go into lessons? Maybe there are some people who are not able to get out of the house very much, or are around with young children a lot, but could promise to pray for you every Wednesday lunchtime while you do your lunchtime group.

Example prayer points for a handout or prayer letter

For your local schools

- For the **staff**, the **pupils** and all other workers in the schools.
- For **churches/individuals** to pray specifically for their school.
- For **justice** in all areas of school life.

For the education system

- For those involved in **making decisions** about education, both locally and nationally.
- For future developments in **national educational policies**.

- For all **Christian organisations** seeking to strengthen the Christian voice in our schools.
- For all those working for the project.

12

Church and School

We have to ask the question today, when a fundamental part of our society is under such stress and pressure, and education is in danger of meltdown, how can the church respond? . . . There has to be the understanding, that the world is an arena in which Christians have to be active. Not only do we have to be active in it, but it's our primary focus of calling. (Andy Hickford, *Meltdown in Schools*, The Stapleford Centre 2001)

Building bridges between churches and schools is a phrase which is bandied around a lot, and it has always been part of our objectives at Leeds Faith In Schools to try to achieve. The excellent book *Generation to Generation* from Scripture Union and Fanfare deals with this issue in much greater depth than I can give it credit for here. It includes 20 practical ideas of how churches can be involved in school; similarly the SMN (Schools Ministry Network) booklet *Support Your Local School* (a guide to opportunities for church involvement in schools) is also helpful in this way.

So I want to give you a few real stories of how churches from different backgrounds have become connected with schools.

Bob Fry

Bob is the pastor of New Life Community Church in Rawdon, which is in the suburbs of Leeds. I asked him about the way that his church is connecting with the local schools.

'Connecting with local schools is a very high priority for our church. McDonald's used to use the slogan 'Happy Kids = Happy Parents' and we are finding that to be true. We are starting to reach families simply by reaching their children, and the best way to do that is through schools. We recently put on a family fun day at a local pub and all the young people that we have had contact with through the schools came with their parents, who were so excited and thankful that we had put on this day for them.

'There are several ways that we have done this. We now have three drop-ins after school on a Wednesday, Thursday and Friday. It is a sort of coffee bar (not that young people drink coffee!). Some of it is slightly structured in a similar way to a youth group, but one of them is completely unstructured – we just have a playstation, table football, air hockey and a few games lying about. The young people come in and hang out and just use our time and equipment to do that. I wouldn't say they are believing, but they do certainly belong, and if we ask them to do things in church maybe on a Sunday morning amazingly most of them will turn up and help us.

'We now have 60 young people from local schools, both primary and secondary, who come into our church building every week. The barriers have been broken down, and they don't have problems with Christians and churches any more because they feel they belong. It has also been great for our relationships with our local schools.

'You should have seen the teachers' faces when we started giving out £5 notes in the assembly!'

One of the more radical things that our church did was to hand over £1,000 (£5 for every Year 9 pupil at one of our local schools) to raise funds for Hope HIV! The young people were given the money with the option of either giving the money straight back or investing it or using it to raise more money. You should have seen the teachers' faces when we started giving out £5 notes in the assembly! It was a great opportunity and we got some good press coverage from it, and the young people were empowered and motivated to raise money for charity – all because our church members were generous enough to put up the money in the first place!

'Our latest news is that we have just been given five free PCs and we are going to start a homework club. Two of our local primary schools don't have homework clubs at the moment, so that will only deepen further our relationships with the schools and we are looking forward to it. I have also become a governor of one of the local schools and several of our church members volunteered to help listen to readers for one morning a week, which the school really appreciates.'

Jo Stow

Jo is the youth minister at St Augustine's Church in Harehills, Leeds – an inner city Catholic parish. I asked her, 'How have you built bridges between church and school?'

'I approached the Catholic high schools in Leeds on the basis that we have got young people from our parish in their

school. I asked the schools if volunteers and myself could come in and serve them while at school. I have found that Catholic schools are dead keen for you to help out, especially when they know that you are employed by a Catholic parish.

'There is one lad in particular I have got to know both in the parish and in school and that has helped enormously. Being able to see him in both places has really helped my relationship with him and his family.

'Because I am Catholic there is no difficulty in getting into school and the staff are generally very welcoming, but after six months in the job I am beginning to realise that the main issue is that "Catholic kids" have "heard it all before". Most have had Catholic teachings from birth or since entering education. They often know all the answers, and so coming with something fresh to catch their attention and make it more real to them is definitely a challenge! Helping them to the point of entering a real relationship with God and "not just head knowledge" is both my main task and greatest challenge in school!'

Peter Jackson

Peter is the chair of governors and the vicar of St Luke's, Holbeck, an inner city parish with a church school connected historically, like many other Anglican parishes around the UK.

'I wear two hats when in school and I have a poster that says that! The staff know that they are able to talk to me as a governor or as the vicar and I am careful not to confuse those roles. I spend nearly a day a week in school doing an open drop-in for parents and teachers every week as well as assemblies and lessons. The church also does services

with the whole school every Christmas and Easter and church visits from the school RE groups. When I am in school now, I am part of school life and I am accepted as part of the furniture, which is great! A school like St Luke's is an oasis for the parents and kids in a really difficult area, and because it is an oasis I obviously want my church and Jesus to be central to that. I have had the privilege of leading a few adults to faith and helped them find a home in our church, which could not have been done without our church being central to school life and the community.

'I was asked to pray for a Moslem woman the other day, as she saw me as the holy man.'

'When I am in school I always say "just grab me if you need me" or the "school can find me if you want me" and this happens often. I was asked to pray for a Moslem woman the other day, as she saw me as the holy man, which was a great privilege. I see the pastoral care of the school as partly my responsibility as the local vicar, and it is great to help out.

Tony Pullin says:

I have a vision where each church is shot through with a passion for Jesus; where a passion for the lost fills our lives and, together, we live for the gospel; praying, sacrificing, laughing and weeping together. I have a vision where each church is seamlessly a part of the community, and the only way to tell the difference is the hallmark of the life of Jesus; where the kingdom is touching every corner of society. (*Compass* magazine, Spring 2002)

Working with Churches Together and groups of churches

I am grateful to Abi Monteith (a full-time schools worker) for the following tips.

'It is really important to connect with the local churches, as they will support you both financially and in prayer. This can be hard work but it's definitely worth it! My experience is that the local Churches Together agreed to financially support my work as a schools worker in their area, but I am not employed by any of them directly.

'Basically, you have to be prepared to go to a few committee meetings and be interested in what is going on with the churches in the area, so you can give your two minutes of feedback on what you are doing. It's really important to keep them up to date with what you are doing. Many churches think you are the answer to all their "lack of youth in the church" problems and will only measure your success with "bums on seats" unless they actually know what you are doing in school.

'I found it helpful to write an update report for every Churches Together meeting which said the facts of what I'd been doing for the last couple of months and any stories that occurred. I also put prayer requests on that. The report would go to the vicars and other people present at the CT meetings and it was up to them how they distributed it. Some would copy it to their congregations; others to their PCC and others just put it at the bottom of a very big pile. (You have to be careful what you write because you never know who it might get passed to!)

'Try and get local church leaders on your side. It's good for them to get to know you as a person as well as know about what you are doing. The better relationship you have *with the local vicars the more helpful they will be to you in the future.*

'You do have to be careful, as you will probably end up being invited to speak at church services, meetings and other things. It's important that you are seen by the congregations and that you can tell them personally what you are doing as they will warm to you and become more interested in what you do. You do have to be careful though not to be put upon too much. Remember your main job is to be in the schools taking Jesus to the kids, not being stuck in church buildings, but it is definitely worthwhile investing some of your time in the churches.

'Prayer support is vital. I wrote to all the vicars in the area explaining who I was and my need for a specific prayer. I asked if they had a prayer group at the church that would want to support a certain school. It's really important that you can ask for a specific prayer request that will not be passed onto whole congregations. I sent a tear-off slip that they could send me back with the details of the contact person and which school they would support. I now write a prayer letter every couple of months for the specific schools and send them to the relevant groups. I didn't have a massive response to the letter: about four churches replied. The main problem as always is knowing who to contact in a church, as the vicar is normally too busy to remember. If you can get other key contacts in the church it will be really helpful to you.

'The other main people you should be friends with are the chairperson and secretary of Churches Together, because if you have their support they will really push your cause and make life easier and more effective for you!'

13

Christian Focus Weeks

Having a week with a visiting band, theatre group or sports team can be an effective way of raising the profile of Christianity in and around school. I have really enjoyed these exciting mad weeks. As a part of a complete schools work strategy, a week like this can be an amazing opportunity for seeing fruit from all those seeds sown in school. They can, however, be a recipe for disaster!

Here are a few tips that may help the Focus Week go a bit smoother.

- The first thing to find out is whether the Christian young people, local churches and teachers in the school want this week, and will the school let you have it?
- Plan it with young people, not for young people.
- If you have a group of visitors in mind to come, make sure you have seen them work and know them well. Get a video, info pack and even references if you feel the school may ask that of you.
- Will the group need accommodation? How much will they charge?

- Find a senior staff member who can be your best advert for the week, and who is really keen to push it.

- Get a group of prayer partners who will cover you before and during the week.

- Plan ahead! These weeks take a lot of planning, and I would advise at least six weeks' notice is needed to organise it effectively.

- Remember that certain times of the school year are not worth considering i.e. the week before Christmas and exam time.

- Do the visitors need to be in one place all week (i.e. the hall) and have the young people come to them? This may be helpful if they have a lot of equipment.

- Get a timetable of lessons including room numbers and all the details you will need. Be careful of duplication – have the group seen that class before?

- Ask the visitors what their expectations are for this week. Grill them!

- If you are thinking of holding a youth event on, say, the Friday night, do you need to sell tickets? Can the group do a taster on the Thursday lunchtime? Will there be a talk and appeal (out of school time)? If so make it clear; do not get young people there by hiding that fact.

- Sometimes it is more effective to invite young people 'to find out more', than it is to ask them, 'Come forward if you want to be a Christian now.' Young people often need to belong first, before they believe.

- If you are looking to challenge people to find out more, sort out the follow-up now, not afterwards! Get Alpha groups, CUs or cells ready to go the week afterwards and give out invitations on the Friday night to those who are interested.

14
Teamwork

Back in 1994, when I started with Leeds Faith In Schools, I was the only schools worker and there were very few youth workers around. So I did sometimes feel a bit like the Lone Ranger, going into schools shooting a silver bullet for Jesus and then legging it off on my own.

It was a pretty lonely job, and after a while I felt that I needed to gather a team together. I was desperate for other colleagues and I was really thankful when Rob, Nicola and other workers and volunteers came along. But then I also realised I enjoyed being on my own, because doing my own thing, being in charge of my own time and doing the schools work *I wanted to do* had its advantages, and I wasn't naturally a team player! I also realised I had my own limitations and baggage that I had brought with me in everything that I did. In order to be healthy myself and to have healthy youth work I needed to work towards a team.

At first I found working as part of a team stressful, but it became more natural to me as I saw the joys and pains of working with a great team in Leeds. I am now absolutely convinced that people who don't work in teams are simply not presenting an important part of God's heart to whoever they are speaking to, or living their lives with. I also thought (fool-ishly!) that it would be easier for me to work with people who are similar to me: people who have the same gifts, maybe the same interests and almost the same personality types. But then I woke up and realised what a nightmare that would be. Imagine a team of Lee Jacksons running around the place!

A team is quite simply 'a group of individuals working for a common purpose'. That means that individuals have different gifts to bring to a team. This is something that really needs to be celebrated and not seen as a threat just because we do things in a different way. A team is there to achieve a purpose but you're also there to get on and have fun together, to relate as human beings. Young people soon pick up the strengths and weaknesses of your team. The strong leader can make or break an organisation simply because they are so busy forging ahead they have left a trail of destruction behind them.

'The most talented individuals in the organisation going off in different directions will seldom reach the same height they would if they joined forces and synergised their efforts.' (Larry Oldman)

There are lots of team training books and internet resources you can check up on, and in fact most residential organisa-tions will do team training for you if you have a group of people that you want to train either at work or in a church situation.

Help each other to be right not wrong

A business came up with the following model for team-work:

Look for new ways to make new ideas work, not for the reasons they won't. If in doubt check it out and don't make negative assumptions about each other. Help each other win and take pride in each other's victories. Speak positively about each other and about your organisation at every opportunity, maintaining a positive mental attitude no matter what the circumstances. Act with initiative and courage and do everything with enthusiasm because it is contagious. Share the glory, but most of all love what you do and have fun.

This is a set of values which I think most youth work organisations and churches should adopt. Teams are the most exciting and the most frustrating things in the world. The fact is that teamwork is here to stay and we'd better get it working for us and not against us!

Linda Harding says that good teams:

- set targets
- monitor performance
- promote and maintain communication
- manage change within the team
- develop and train members
- steward resources
- manage relationships with other groups
- learn from experience
- monitor and manage environment
- build relationships

Here is a simple way to monitor your teamwork at work or at church. Complete the following chart when you have finished an activity. Think about how the group worked as a team before you complete the chart.

Rate yourself on a scale:

1   = Helped team
2   = OK
3   = Not helpful to team

[Activity]	[Date]	
	Notes	Score
Overall contribution to the group process		
Individual effort		
Co-operation		
Reliability		
Completion of work on time		
Leadership in team		
Value as team member		
Involvement in activity		

15

Safety and Child Protection

Working within a school environment is easier in many ways, as far as safety and child protection is concerned, because you are working with systems that are already in place. As you work in a school, especially doing voluntary work like lunchtime clubs and sports clubs, make sure you ask about and are aware of things such as fire procedures, bullying policies and child protection procedures. There are probably lots of documents produced at a school level for these, so don't be afraid to ask for them. Here are a few tips which will help you and the young people in your care to be safer while working in and around school.

Establish a discipline procedure

Christians shouldn't be walkovers; we should have clear discipline procedures. Unruly or unsafe behaviour needs to be dealt with in the correct manner. Many people use the idea of the football referee, as young people seem to understand and respond to this very well. In our Rock Solid box we often have a red and a yellow card: a yellow card is a warning if someone is deliberately being abusive, disruptive or unsafe; a red card means a 'one match ban'. In other words they will be asked to leave immediately and not allowed to come back to the club the next week. Young people will often test boundaries, so it is important that you have boundaries that you are able to establish and reinforce clearly.

All lunchtime clubs should have a mixture of male and female leaders. Is there a teacher or member of staff in the school that would be happy to come to a lunchtime club or group? Often they will only pop in for a few minutes but knowing there is a teacher nearby, or attached to a voluntary club, would remind the young people that the club is within the school environment and the school rules still apply. Be very aware of the room you are working in and the potential hazards that are there, i.e. trailing wires, things sticking out of the walls, desks and chairs. Fun does not have to be unsafe.

Common sense

Make sure you sign in at the reception desk and wear your visitor's badge. It is important that you are seen as a genuine member of staff or visitor to the school and not as a potential drug dealer (as one lunchtime supervisor thought I was!).

Youth work is made easier and safer with a few common-sense policies that you can put into place. On the whole, avoid situations where you are alone with a young person, especially of the opposite sex. Make sure that a door is open in the classroom or walk out and speak to them in an open place. Never agree to meet a young person without someone's knowledge, and always agree to meet them in a public place, which is fairly easily done in a school situation. Sometimes in a school environment I believe it is wise for male leaders to appear a little colder to girls in school. This doesn't mean you can't smile and be nice to people, it just means that you need to make sure you keep your distance, especially from teenage girls. A hug is often a way for allegations to be brought, especially from vulnerable girls in school. Remember, this is to protect both young people and workers. The implications of a false allegation can be as damaging as a real one in terms of the work you seek to do, so take care!

The National Criminal Record Bureau started work in March 2002. This is used for checking the records of all paid and volunteer workers with children and young people. A number of area youth and voluntary organisations plus many church headquarters are acting as umbrella groups to administer these checks. There may be a small administrative fee for paid workers, but volunteers should be free.

Most youth work organisations, schools, dioceses and local authorities have Child Protection Courses, which you could attend. These are often only a few hours long and are very helpful in understanding the full picture around safety and child protection.

Below is the text of a card which our volunteers and workers use at Rock Solid clubs, as a very basic guideline on dealing with allegations of abuse, or suspected abuse.

It is the policy of Leeds Faith In Schools to safeguard children and young people by protecting them from physical, sexual, and emotional harm. This card is designed for you to keep with you.

WHAT HAPPENS IF YOU SUSPECT A CHILD
OR YOUNG PERSON IS BEING ABUSED?

1. Immediately tell your Rock Solid leader. If they are unavailable or implicated, tell a member of staff.
2. Write down the facts as soon as possible and give a copy to the Rock Solid leader, project manager, or staff member.
3. Ensure that the child has access to an independent adult.
4. Ensure that there is no immediate danger to the child.

WHAT IF A CHILD DISCLOSES ABUSE TO
YOU BY SOMEONE ELSE?

1. Advise that you will offer support but that you must pass the information on. Do not promise confidentiality.
2. Allow the child to speak without interruption, accepting what is said.
3. Alleviate the child's feelings of guilt and isolation.
4. Let the child know what you are going to do next and you'll let them know what happens.
5. Same steps as 1 to 4 as suspecting a child is being abused.

IF YOU RECEIVE AN ALLEGATION ABOUT
ANY ADULT, OR ABOUT YOURSELF:

1. Immediately inform the Rock Solid leader, project manager, or a member of staff.
2. Record the facts as you know them and file a copy to the Rock Solid leader, project manager, or staff member.
3. Try to ensure that no one is placed in a position which could cause further compromise.

You MUST refer; you MUST NOT investigate.

CONTACT NUMBERS: [list relevant numbers]

16

Small Groups in Schools

One of the most exciting and frustrating things about being in ministry or being a schools worker is when you are told how good things are elsewhere! I visited a church to talk about the work I do in school, and a woman came up to me over the tea and coffee and started sharing about how there had been a 'mini revival' in one school in Leeds and they now had over 100 young people in the classroom every single week singing songs, worshipping and praying to Jesus. It left me with two options: I could get excited about it or I could get depressed by it. It was as simple as that! I did get excited by it and it did drive me on to do new things in school, but it also frustrated me because I looked at my groups in school and wondered what the future held for them.

So I started to ask the question, 'Are groups in school important, and if so what do we do about them and what format should they take?' Here, I will give you some details of different kinds of groups I have come across. Maybe your local school has another group which you can add to this list.

Underground

Leeds has 43 high schools and 270 primary schools, and during eight years of networking in the city I have only come across three Christian Unions in the whole of Leeds! This is partly due to the fact that Leeds has less Christian input than many major cities, but I believe it is also the simple fact that the *traditional* Christian Union's day has gone. This was brought home to me in the first few weeks of my job.

A group of lively Christian teenagers from a local church approached me and the youth pastor and asked if we could help them with their school Christian Union group. So we arranged a meeting and listened to them sharing about where they were at. They said, 'No one shows up, or we get laughed at. We have the doors slammed by people during the meeting, we have things thrown at us and we get called names like Jesus freak, Bible basher, etc.'

They turned to me and the youth pastor and asked what we thought they should do about it, and I (being full of wisdom, careful thought and consideration) answered immediately, 'Close it down!' This took a few of them by surprise. Then we spent the next couple of hours dreaming about what we could do and how we could relaunch it in some way. So we set about doing a poster campaign, which consisted of a picture of a dead, rotten fish with the words 'The Christian Union is dead' written above it. These posters were put all around school and caused quite a stir – even some of the teachers thought it was a campaign by people to discredit the Christian Union.

We did a 'disciples in the upper room' thing, where we decided to go underground. The result was amazing. We started putting the underground symbol on the posters and changed the posters from 'The Christian Union is dead' into 'The Underground is praying for you!'. We started meeting once or twice a week before school to pray for the school and to meet and worship together. This lively youth group brought in one or two other people from different churches, and they got so fired up about the school, and what they wanted God to do in the school, they decided to organise a school mission. I can still see fruit from that mission today.

Prayer groups

The Underground was a little more than an extension of a church youth group and a good prayer group. Young people were up at 7.00 am to come and pray for their friends in school, so something was going on there. This helped me to understand that if young people can meet and pray together in a relevant safe environment then exciting things can happen. I hear of stories at the moment where prayer groups are springing up around schools and God is moving on the teachers and the pupils alike!

Here's a letter sent to www.24-7prayer.com

'At the 24–7 conference in April, my brother came up the front and told everyone that God wanted him and his mate to start praying each lunchtime at our school. That's been going on non-stop since January. He said he was to not stop until God started to do something in St Edwards, with teachers and pupils. Well God *is* doing something BIG! What he's put on our hearts, and the plans he has for our school, is mind blowing! Non-Christians' eyes are more open to what God is doing and who he is to them. Teachers are supporting God's wild plans!

The Christian Union which was once so PANTS has now got so much life and so many people who are hungry to come every Tuesday lunchtime.

'Today we had an all-day Prayer Room in the middle of the sixth form block because of the international day of prayer. Loads of people came to check it out and spend their free time praying. There was healing, prophesy and vision.

'We hope to get a permanent prayer room for our school. The only reason why Denise and I are staying on is to see God move in this school. He promised a wave of his power to sweep through and we want to see it. He is moving in the younger generation, so we thought to encourage you and others. God bless and keep going.'

Rock Solid

I'd heard about Rock Solid at a youth workers' conference and became quite interested in it as it seemed to be a great package for the 11- to 14-year-olds. Then when my friend John Hawksworth moved to Leeds he got me even more excited as he started telling me how he'd adapted his Rock Solid club in his old job to become a little bit more school friendly. We got talking and eventually we launched a Rock Solid club in school and I launched one or two others around the schools in Leeds.

Rock Solid is a whole package of material that you can buy into for a small monthly charge. It has been researched and developed by Youth For Christ for the 11+ age group, now acknowledged as the 'key group' to target. It is designed for an evening group, usually two hours long, but I felt that it could be used in schools, with a bit of stream-lining. There are now eight or more Rock Solid Clubs in Leeds and I have seen God help these groups grow into a great foundation for ministry in schools.

The advantages of Rock Solid are:

- It is well researched and written and gives a year's material, term by term.
- It takes away the pressure of planning every week from scratch.
- You can spend more time building relationships and looking to build the future i.e. small groups/residentials, etc.
- It allows kids to feel part of a bigger network, especially if you use membership cards.
- Every session has a theme, usually a life issue to deal with, i.e. friends, bullying, being popular etc., so it is well suited to non-Christians and is much more attractive than a 'What is the Bible' to a Year 8 pupil.
- Youth for Christ encourages team development before you buy into it, so it helps you think about a team before you launch Rock Solid.

I found one of the best things about doing Rock Solid in school is it allowed me to plan ahead and have a framework to work from. It stopped me having those panicky 'what am I going to do in the Christian group in school tomorrow' thoughts, that I used to live with. I think I had been through just about every Christian youth manual and programme that was around. Having Rock Solid helped me to allow time to think of the young people and where I was going. Having a programme structure to work from seems to free your mind up to think of the bigger picture rather than just the details all the time.

The other exciting thing about Rock Solid is that it encourages a great team dynamic. It is quite easy for one person to lead a Christian Union, but Rock Solid is pretty crazy and it needs at least three or four people of different abilities and skills to do it, and this is more healthy for the young people as they get to see men and women working together to produce something which is relevant to them.

By the time this book comes out we will have published a supplement to the Rock Solid manual to make it more friendly for schools. If you are interested in Rock Solid then contact YFC on 0121 5508055 or check out www.YFC.co.uk.

Rock Solid, like any other programme for groups in school, has its ups and downs, its pros and cons, but I feel that it has been one of the most effective things that I have done in my time as a schools worker, and it certainly helped build the bridges between churches and schools – plus the kids just love it!

We are all looking for God to move in the school situation, and one of the reasons I tried to develop Rock Solid was so that we could have a foundation in place. I suppose in a way I tried to develop Rock Solid to prepare for revival and what I believe God will do in the future in this nation.

Justice groups

Emma Flint has started developing these groups.

'We seem to struggle enthusing young people to get excited or passionate about anything at school. Well, that's what I've found! Especially when it involves giving up lunchtime! But certain issues seem to capture young people's sense of injustice, and as Christian youth workers it should be our responsibility to harness these feelings.

'Most schools that we work in do not have a Christian Union, and if they do, the majority of the school wouldn't be seen dead at it. So there is the problem of how do we get God's heart across to these young people who do not believe. It seems to me that if young people see us in different contexts other than RE lessons, and they know that we are Christians, they will soon see what God cares about. We all know that God talks about compassion and justice for the poor, pretty much more than anything else in the Bible. So it makes sense that we should spend a lot of time doing this too. Kids want to know that they can make a difference, as most of the time they don't believe that they can. We can show them just how much God loves the world and how much they can make a difference by getting involved in justice issues.

'One example is, that after a sixth form conference, some sixth formers felt passionate about the Jubilee 2000 Drop the Debt campaign that they had learned about. The speaker had given them specific and simple ways to campaign and to get their friends involved. So after the conference, the teacher and I arranged a number of lunchtime meetings where the young people could find out more about the campaign, and begin a petition in the school, informing different year groups through assemblies.

'There do seem to be certain issues that grab kids' attention. I have found that these are to do with things that they spend a lot of time thinking about in their own lives. The main example being Fair Trade, as it involves food, especially chocolate, and child labour in sweatshops as this involves the clothes they wear and people their own age being treated unfairly. Make sure the young people are given a practical way in which they can make a difference and that their own lifestyle is challenged.

'I have done many assemblies, lessons and clubs on issues now, especially Fair Trade, and have found that they are an *amazing way to bring in my faith and how radical the God we follow is.'*

Cell groups

We have seen a few cell groups develop in the school environment in Leeds, and I am also hearing stories from around the country about this. A cell, in biological terms, is the basic unit of structure within a living human body. A body is comprised of cells that have been formed and patterned by God. Every one of these cells is unique yet they all function together to keep the body healthy and co-ordinated. It is important to realise that as a body grows larger, cells have been reproducing and multiplying on the inside. 1 Corinthians 12:27 tells us: 'You are the body of Christ, and each one of you is a part of it.' As the church, the body of Christ, we are also a living organism. The way we grow is by each member fulfilling their role in relation to other members. As we find each other we begin to function together, multiply and grow the church. We cannot function in isolation.

A cell is the 'basic building block' of church. We all need relationships with people we can identify with and who can help us in our Christian walk. The cell group is a practical way for us to find true community and, more importantly, participate in it. With cells, we are not limited by the capacity of physical buildings, central church meetings or the skills of a few full-time workers. Cells enable many more young people to be empowered and released to reach their friends with the good news about Jesus.

Many churches and youth ministries have a form of small group attached to a main event, but with cells the focus is changed from the rather large 'congregation plus

pastor', or 'youth work plus leader', to the small group of
like-minded people loving God, caring for one another and
reaching out to those who as yet do not know God. Youth
cells are exactly the same: a group of people with similar
needs and interests meeting together regularly to worship,
help each other and reach out.

A youth cell is:
• small – between 6 and 12 people
• temporary – the aim of each cell is to grow and multiply
• a place to encounter Jesus
• a place to belong
• a place to grow
• a place to give
• a place to reach out
(From the excellent Sublime youth cells website
www.sublime.hants.org.uk)

There is one particularly thriving Christian Union group in
Leeds at a church school, and off the back of the Christian
Union there have been a few cell groups started up. These
have become more and more relevant to non-Christian kids
mainly through friends inviting other friends. You could
say it is planting church in school, as a cell is a living breathing community of believers. The mentoring and peer discipleship which goes hand in hand with the cell group has
been really exciting to see, especially as some of the older
pupils have taken hold of what it means to be a role model
and a mentor to some of the younger people.

Joe who plays in my basketball team is one of these
people. He has been a great role model not only because he
is 6'3" but because he is a follower of Jesus. He introduced
me to a Year 8 lad at a youth event in Leeds, who has since

come to faith through being with a cell and hanging out with people like Joe. That is the stuff that gets me really excited!

The word 'cell' and what it means has threatened many people, especially church leaders. It is important that we don't get frightened off something before we know what it really is. I believe cell groups are the real key to the future shape of church for young people and it is important that we don't throw out the baby with the bathwater and dismiss something before we have even tried it. There are specific youth cell conferences now which deal with some of the deeper issues, if you are interested in finding out more.

Light Lunch

My friend Rob also developed a school group, which is based around food, not surprisingly, as he is known for his food addiction. He called it Light Lunch and basically he bought a kettle and a toaster and provided simply a bit of toast and a cup of tea. Having food around just helps people to relax, it means they can be there for a longer time not having to queue up for their lunch and helps people to get to know each other better. Where young people have to come out of the house early because their mum and dad work, you can actually provide a Christian breakfast club.

After-school clubs

Tony Blair has been promoting the idea of after-school clubs, and some churches and Christian groups are starting to take up this opportunity, so investigate the funding opportunities that are there. The government might pay you to do your work, which is nice!

Other kinds of groups, which you may not have thought of, include a group for pupils that are at risk of exclusion: the school will know these young people and will be glad of any help. A learning mentor is a person who especially helps young people and the family to cope with the pressures of life and school, helping with the pastoral, motivational and special needs of a selected group of young people within the school. Could you offer your help to them?

How about a sports group? You could watch a football match or you could start a club: basketball, football or tiddlywinks.

Dylan Goggs, a schools worker from Bradford, was a break-dancer and a couple of years ago he started break-dance classes with some of the young people that he worked with. And as he took on his new role as a schools worker in Bradford, he has continued to use break-dancing as a tool to get to know young people and also serve the school by offering extra-curricular activities. Obviously not everyone can teach break-dancing, but it is a great example of using your gifts to do something different in the school environment. A lot of Dylan's time is taken up doing break-dance classes and it has become a very successful part of his ministry in one of the most difficult schools in the country.

I have done many DJ workshops in schools, showing kids in RE, music, drama and other lessons what a DJ does and how that relates to my faith. It is great to see kids realise that Christians can be break-dancers and DJs and not just vicars.

Then of course there are arts groups: maybe the art teacher would let you use the art studio so that you can try to develop some pieces of artwork? There are many different things that you can do. Just be creative and use the skills that God has given you.

A few guidelines

If you have decided what kind of group you want to start, there are a few steps that you can take:

- Take your time, think and pray for a few weeks about the whole thing to try and get both your and God's perspective on it.
- Try to gather a team to help you: the most important thing is to make sure that when you start a group you can sustain it.
- Once you have spoken to your team and have decided roughly when you want to do it, what time of the day and what day of the week, decide whether it is a weekly, fortnightly or monthly group that you are trying to run.
- Finally – publicity. Get some good posters with catchy titles and the name of your group (if you have decided on one). Try to avoid cheesy Christian artwork or jargon.
- Maybe do an assembly to advertise the group and spread the word.
- Launch the group with a party, plenty of free chocolate, freebies, maybe special guests and extra staff to help.
- Enjoy yourself!

I will finish this chapter with an email I received that blew me away:

'After running two holiday clubs on consecutive years in the village where we live, I felt God was calling me to set up an after school Christian club in the school where I work. After

much prayer and consideration of the best times and days, we started the club (my husband the Methodist minister, and I) and agreed that it would be worth running if 6 or more came. The first week we had 16 children out of a possible 55, and within a year the numbers had grown to 35 children each week. This is a very deprived area socially and I think many parents were glad to leave their kids at school for an extra hour's free childcare. However, as time went on the word spread and the kids grew to love the club, some even asking to come to school on Wednesdays so that they could come to Kingdom Kids, even when they were ill.

'We are now in our third year and still we have more than 50 per cent of the possible intake of children and they absolutely love it!

'Why is it so successful? We have pondered this many times and feel it is a combination of:

1. *Lots of prayer and clear guidance from God to start and continue the club. We have reviewed it each year, believing nothing should continue for the sake of it but only if God wants it to.*

2. *Many of the kids in our care are not listened to by adults at home and have very disturbed backgrounds. When they come to KK they always have a warm welcome and we take an interest in them as people and try to build relationships with them. We are a living witness to the love of Jesus and possibly the only Christians they know. As one child said to me, "You follow Jesus and we follow you."*

3. *We have loads of fun. They especially love crafts they can take home each week, which they can't do with*

normal school work, and lots of wild action songs and silly games.

4. *It is in their school and immediately after school ends so they are on familiar territory. Also as they know me from school we have no problems with discipline, as they are very respectful of me. They also know my husband really well from his assemblies, etc.*

5. *We have always sought to reach out to the kids for themselves and not to get to their parents, though with much of the literature we have sent home we know the gospel is going to homes too.*

'*Over the three years we have been privileged to see more than 50 kids make a commitment to Jesus, and we believe many will go on with him and grow in their faith. Sadly, we have not been very supported by the local church people who feel that unless it is in the church building it is not valid or proper "church", but nonetheless we have been so encouraged to see God's hand in its success. Even the teachers are amazed and slightly confused as to its success; we have more kids than the rest of the school clubs put together! We are moving this summer and the club will end as no one is prepared to take it on, but we aren't worried about that. We just leave all the young souls in his care and trust him to grow this new generation of leaders, evangelists and theologians!*

PS This village has long been renowned for its curse upon children and was the last place in the UK to have child sacrifices. When we first arrived here we heard of many untimely deaths of children. Over the years these have stopped and we feel that God has turned the curse into a great blessing. This has not been easy work and we have been under a lot of attack as we are storming the powers of darkness, but ultimately God's will is and will be done.'

Finally, remember groups outside of school lesson time are classed as voluntary i.e. the staff and young people choose to go there. This gives you a little more freedom to be open and direct about your faith, but as always it is not a licence to preach.

Further reading

Running Christian Groups in Secondary Schools by Simon Barker and Bruce Lockhart (Scripture Union, 1999).

17

Residential Courses

Since the tragic situation in Royds School where two girls died in the river when walking as part of their course, residential trips have been in the news usually for bad reasons. In the light of other tragic incidents, I have heard teachers say that they are not interested in taking residentials at all now. As schools have to keep developing their residential programme, there will be lots of scope for volunteers to help to supervise on school trips and residential courses in the future.

Here are a few residential courses and trips: maybe you could list one or two more that happen in your local schools.

- Outward bound residential – a classic!
- Year 7 Induction or Year 6 Leaving – specifically for bonding purposes.
- Educational trips, where the students are taken away in order to study a particular subject.
- Christian residentials, which you may see as part of your strategy for reaching and keeping young people you meet in a school environment. Maybe a Christian

Union or Rock Solid residential where you take them away for the weekend. You can be obviously explicit about the Christian background and not be restricted by school policy on visiting religious groups.

- Then there are the plain old fun residentials.
- There are also day trips: a lot of RE departments have class pilgrimages to various places like Abbeys and Cathedrals. There are also theatre trips, usually to Stratford to see Shakespeare, or trips to museums like the Royal Armouries or National Film and Photography museum, and my favourite – the London trip!
- There are also sport-related trips – rugby tours and football away matches and competitions. One of my schools got into the final of a netball competition a few years ago and it ended up being a three-day residential.

It is often frustrating in schools work not to be able to spend long with the young people, but a residential is a great opportunity to spend chunks of time. I went on a Disneyland Paris trip, where we were on a coach for what

---

'The ministry of the sick bag made it an unforgettable journey!'

---

seemed like for ever. I asked the teacher which young people she thought would be a problem, and they were sitting around the back seat (of course), so I deliberately went to sit on the back seat with them and spent almost two days on a coach, chatting with them, getting to know them, having a laugh and trying to sleep while they flicked sweets at me. The ministry of the sick bag made it an unforgettable journey!

I find it amazing the difference it makes when you get back to school the next week and the young people that you saw at clubs, or in lessons and assemblies, are suddenly your friends because they know you so well now. They'd hung out with you, had meals with you, and it was a great opportunity just to let them know that Christians are quite normal people, and we don't all wear sandals with or without socks!

You get to know the staff as well, as obviously you can be a great help to them during the day – and during the night when the young people have decided to have midnight snacks and swap rooms, and all the usual things that go on at residentials. An extra pair of hands is great, and because I went as a youth worker I was able to be a bit like their big brother, rather than like a teacher having to discipline them. I gained a lot of respect from the teachers, because they could see that I was genuine, and we used to have a good banter with each other in the staff room. It has to be said that residentials are usually quite exhausting as you are on call pretty much all of the time, but they are also great fun and well worth the effort.

It is important to keep the distinction that you are not a teacher in those environments, but not to the point where you undermine a teacher. You have to go with whatever disciplinary decision a teacher makes but you can be distinctly different. One of the ways I used to do this was to go and eat with the kids on their table at mealtime. It is usually a bit of a free-for-all when the chips come out, but it's great fun to chat about what they are into, what they do outside of school, and their home situation, enabling you to know them better. Even if I can't make it for the whole time, I try to go for a day in the middle of a residential to walk with them in the afternoon, maybe have tea with them, and then do a little disco for their last night, which usually goes down well. I was always seen as someone who brought more fun to the residential.

A lot of schools workers also have some great times on specifically Christian residentials, where the young people have not only made decisions to follow Jesus at that time but also learnt to pray out loud and to support each other. There are some organisations that can help you, such as the Fort Rocky programme at Youth for Christ. This is a weekend that is put on for you, so all you have to do is take the kids there. There are also venue-finding agencies that can advise you on organising your own residential, including insurance, programming, etc.

Below is a suggested programme for when you are organising your own residential and you want some Christian input. A good thing to bear in mind is that natural conversations prodded in the right direction during the weekend can be more effective than any ten-minute talk.

Draft Programme

Friday

   4.30 Leave school
   6.00 Arrive settle in, etc
   7.00 Food!
   8.00 Meeting, games, warm ups, etc
  10.00 Short night walk followed by supper
  10.45 Mellow time
  11.00 Sleep – you'll need it!

Saturday

   8.00 Breakfast
   8.30 Leaders' meeting / free time
   9.30 Activity session
  12.30 Packed lunch
   1.30 Activity session

6.00 Food
7.30 Sharing about the day
9.30 Cabaret
10.30 Supper and chill-out time
11.00 Sleep

Sunday

8.00 Breakfast
8.30 Leaders' meeting / free time
9.30 Group walk / activity
1.00 Lunch and pack stuff
2.30 Last teaching session – invite kids to group in school
4.30 Leave
6.00 Arrive back at school

If you are organising your own residential, a healthy view of finances is always helpful. Depending on what kind of area you are working in, don't be afraid to charge the kids the full rate, as most young people and parents are quite used to paying out for the residentials. If you are doing it with a lunchtime group or Christian Union, involving them in raising funds to reduce the cost of the residential is just as good as the residential itself. It empowers the young people and it makes them own it (and it means they'll turn up).

Plan ahead, as often you will have to book a year in advance, especially for weekends. I once organised a residential where only one person signed up to it! Sometimes this happens, and there are a thousand reasons why young people do or don't want to go, so don't take it personally.

Send me a postcard!

18

Sixth Form Conferences

I am grateful to Emma Flint for the following material on a new development in schools work.

Schools are required to provide RE for sixth form students, but the reality is that it is difficult to fit this into their already full timetable. Schools seem to be going for the idea of a one-day conference each term to try to cover the compulsory RE. This is obviously a big undertaking, but our experience at Leeds Faith In Schools has been that schools welcome any help they can get.

One possibility is to put together a whole pack on sixth form conferences that you as an organisation can provide if you have the people and the resources. Schools will have a budget for this, so may be willing to pay. Another idea is just to get to know the head of sixth form and see where you can help. The main subjects to cover in sixth form RE seem to be Wealth and Poverty, Human Rights and Medical Ethics.

In Leeds, two schools joined together to put on a conference for their sixth form on the theme of 'Wealth and Poverty'. LFIS were very involved in arranging seminar speakers for morning and afternoon sessions as we had contacts that the school did not. We got in touch with all our Christian friends in Leeds who work with people in poverty in some way. This was an amazing opportunity for the sixth formers to discover more of what Christians are doing in our city. We got in people working with asylum seekers, the homeless, a worker for Jubilee 2000 and an ex heroin addict who had become a Christian. The school greatly appreciated the diversity of people we brought in, and it was a lesson for us on effective ways to use our contacts and friends in the school environment.

I think that this sort of conference is going to increase, so we need to think of creative ways of getting involved. Sixth Form is a great place to be a schools worker, as the young people have actually chosen to study and seem genuinely interested in people who have a faith and live by it. The questions will stretch you more than in any other age group, but it is exciting as this is the time that the young people are making a lot of life choices and decisions.

Here is a sample sixth form pack that we pulled together. Please do not copy it but just use it as a guide!

SIXTH FORM CONFERENCE: WEALTH AND POVERTY

Introduction

Due to the expansion of the Leeds Faith In Schools team and the recent success of a sixth form conference for [name] school at Leeds Metropolitan University, we believe we are now in a situation to offer to help organise and run sixth form RE conferences for the schools that we have contact with. It is possible that we could find a venue outside of school or do it within your own school.

We would aim to use a main hall where we would provide a video projector, a screen and any other audio visual equipment that we need, and then we would use several smaller rooms for the seminars, as it is best to work in groups and not just spend the whole day in one large plenary session.

The conference which we delivered at the LMU was on Wealth and Poverty, and debate on this topic seems to be in demand from RE teachers.

We use speakers who are known to us and who we believe are relevant and interactive communicators for the sixth form age group.

The cost

The cost for the sixth form conference is dependent on the cost of speakers. As most people invited by Leeds Faith In Schools represent charities, we would usually work out a rate and suggest a donation from the school.

We would just ask you to remember that Leeds Faith In Schools has no statutory funding and is funded primarily from churches and individuals in Leeds. Therefore a significant donation for our time would be appreciated.

If you have any questions about sixth form conferences please do not hesitate to contact us at the Leeds Faith In Schools office. The address is on the front cover.

Draft Programme

Seminars/workshops – one hour long

The idea is that the young people go to two seminars; one on poverty in this country and one from a global perspective. There will be a chance to ask questions and some group discussion.

Example workshops:

Global

1. LFIS team – what you can do – global citizenship.
2. Drop the Debt Campaign.
3. [name] – their work among the poor.
4. Trade for change. Fair/unfair trade.
5. Christian Aid – their work

Local

6. Homelessness in Leeds.
7. Leeds Asylum – Name of group
8. Drugs in Leeds – caring from a Christian perspective.
9. [name] – an ex drug addict and Big Issue seller who became a Christian.
10. [name] – Christian organisation working with teenage drug addicts and prostitutes.
11. Christians against poverty – group helping people in this country to get out of debt.

Everyone will then meet together to discuss how they respond to what they have heard, and whether there is anything they can follow up as a sixth form or individually.

A proposed timetable

10.00–10.30	Students arrive
10.30–11.15	Plenary Session – Introduction to the day
11.30–12.15	First workshop
12.15– 1.30	Lunch (provided)
1.30– 2.15	Second workshop
2.30– 3.15	Final plenary session and feedback

Other possible topics for future conferences might include:

- The sanctity of life
- What is truth? The meaning of life. What am I here for?
- Is there such a thing as right and wrong?

Resource

You may also want to contact Damaris who offer sixth form conferences to schools all over the country. Visit their website – www.damaris.org.

19
Teachers and Staff

David Blunkett, the Secretary of State for Education, said in December 2000, 'The Education system has nearly experienced meltdown.' The following statistic about teachers is a sure sign of this: '40% of teachers leave the profession within three years of starting' (Spring Prayer Guide, Care For Education, March to May 2002).

The teachers and support staff in schools are under enormous pressure, and with media coverage of failing schools, it seems that people who work in schools seem to be just above 'Attila the Hun' in the public's estimation! One of the most demoralising things for teachers is when, after a hard day at school, they switch on the news as they are having their tea and there is yet another story of something which teachers have been blamed for. It is vitally important that we as schools workers and Christians support the staff in our school. Here are a few tips and ideas for how we can help them.

- In church situations we need to make sure we are praying for staff on a regular basis.
- Make sure we affirm teachers publicly. Don't joke

about their having long holidays; it really isn't very helpful.

- Think of the teachers when you were at school. Did any of them affect you? Do you remember any of them as being really good people? If you do, then thank them and make sure that we are thanking current staff in schools as well, for what they are doing.

- Why not have a church service especially devoted to praying for schools and for staff? Get the teachers in your church to stand up, then lay hands on them and pray for them and for the job that they do.

- Find out when the OFSTED inspections are coming around. Bridge Street Church in Leeds committed themselves to praying every morning throughout an OFSTED inspection, asking God to bless the school and that it would do the best that it could. That meant us getting out of bed slightly earlier than normal, but it made a great difference, I believe, to the morale and to the integrity of our schools work. The staff knew that we were in every morning praying during that difficult time.

- Ring up the teachers, both Christian and non Christian, and ask them for some prayer points.

- Why not stop right now and write down the names of the teachers you know and commit to pray for them on a regular basis? Tell them that you are doing that even if they don't know Jesus yet.

Encourage teachers with stories like this from Pete Gilbert.

'There was the boys' school in East London where the RE teacher was Christian and for two or more years, before having us into the school, he prayed consistently as he stood at the door of his classroom over every child by name as they entered his classroom. When we were finally permitted to take lessons and assemblies it was in richly turned soil and the result was a mini-revival in the school, with dozens and dozens of young lads coming to faith in Christ and starting up a Christian Union on the premises, which to my knowledge continued to serve the gospel in that school for several years following.'

What is a 'good' school?

'Ask me my three main priorities for government, and I tell you; education, education, education.' (Tony Blair, 1 October 1996)

As a governor I see far too much emphasis on positions in league tables by both professionals and parents rather than the growth and attainment of each child from wherever they start. Among those with such an attitude are many Christians. The Government is increasing the capacity for selection which poses a real question about who will take the children whose predictions for 'success' are not that great. They deserve personal fulfilment too! (Ann Holt, Director of Care for Education)

Comments like that from Ann have been a real breath of fresh air for me as I have worked in what are classed as 'good schools' and 'bad schools' mainly due to the great emphasis we place on league tables.

I would like to challenge the viewpoint, especially among the churches, about what is a 'good' or 'bad' school. A school is a school – it has a job to do, some of them do it better than others, some will have greater opportunities to do it better than others, but I believe that as Christians we should be counter-cultural in a society where the negative is often emphasised. It does not encourage staff and pupils to be told theirs is a 'bad school'. I have lost count of the amount of times people have asked me, 'Is that a good school, Lee?' It is about time that Christians just saw schools as schools; collections of people trying to educate and influence and shape the lives of young people. My children are now three years old and I am also going through the discussion of what school they will go to, but the decision I make will be based on several factors and not just the position in a league table or what the local newspaper says about the school. I remember my dad saying that Christians are always radical until it comes to their kids.

I have met some amazing Christians who have deliberately sent their children to a local school rather than making them travel a long way to a so-called good school, and that has shown true commitment to their community. I challenge you now to stop using the phrase 'good' or 'bad school'. It is not our place to judge schools; it is our place to serve them and help them to become better.

20

Becoming a School Governor

An MP was chatting with a senior church leader in Leeds. The church leader asked him how the church could serve the city better, and his immediate response was, 'We need more school governors.' It must be our time to respond to pleas like this.

The governing body of a school has a responsibility to work in partnership with the head teacher and the staff to establish the aims and objectives of the school to ensure that the curriculum is taught in the school, ensure their resources are well deployed, appoint staff, deal with complaints and disciplinary issues, provide an environment which promotes good teaching and learning, continually to seek improvement for all pupils by setting specific targets for all aspects of school life. Being a school governor is demanding voluntary work in the community and Christians with a call to mission and service should be among those taking a share in this task. It is important that there is a proper representation on school governing bodies of those able to speak effectively for Christian beliefs and values and to demonstrate those beliefs and values as they willingly serve the community as an expression of Christian love and commitment.

Each governor acts as a member of the governing body. Individual governors need to remember that they are accountable to one another for their actions as governors. The biblical concept of the whole body working together should not be too hard for the Christian governor to grasp! (Taken from the excellent booklet *Becoming a School Governor – the Christian calling* produced by Care For Education)

Why not prayerfully consider whether you could be a school governor? It is a highly influential and effective way to serve and work in your local school. Anyone over the age of 18 can become a governor. There are many roles that governors undertake, so you don't have to be involved necessarily in the 'hiring and firing' of people. Please contact Care (www.care.org.uk) as they have got some great resources in this area and are keen to seek more representation of the Christian community on governing bodies.

Recently Leeds Faith In Schools was able to continue work in a school in Leeds primarily because of the representation of a Christian governor on the governing body. It was great to see the body of Christ at work in this way.

The challenge to the church is clear, governors are especially well placed to meet it . . . Potential trainee teachers hear a largely negative view of the profession, often from existing teachers struggling to keep up under the pressures. Governors can present a more balanced picture and talk up the value, calling and impact that teachers undoubtedly have. (*Education Update*, Care For Education, January 2002)

21

Hard Questions and Tough Times

'I may not always know what I am talking about but I know I am right!' (Mohammed Ali)

Somewhere in my evangelical history it was impressed upon me that I was meant to defend the truth at all costs and make sure that I win all the arguments for Jesus! I'm sure that I was never taught this but I came away with that impression and I am sure I sounded like Ali in certain situations. 'It's harder to make amends with an offended friend than to capture a fortified city. Arguments separate friends like a gate locked with iron bars' (Proverbs 18:19 NLT).

I am very keen on apologetics and giving a reasoned answer for the things I believe in. But I soon realised in my work in schools that winning an argument can often destroy people and put up more barriers to the Christian faith than break them down. As I look at the stories of Jesus and how he treated people, I feel sure he did a lot of listening and allowed people to vent their frustrations or to put across their point. He spoke in parables that didn't always give the answer but allowed people to work it out for themselves.

Another key to unlocking the church doors for this generation seems to be the style of leadership on Alpha. That came across in the TV series, where leader Paul Cowley was seen to be encouraging questions rather than answering them. 'We have been saying for years that the leaders shouldn't give a talk – simply ask questions,' said Gumbel. One person complained that Cowley had been asked a specific question about the cross, yet didn't give the stock evangelical response. He was very disappointed with Paul who had this wonderful opportunity on national television to answer this question and fluffed it. But he hadn't fluffed it; he'd exercised great restraint and said, 'What do other people think?' The questions are more important than the answers on Alpha courses. The idea seems to be to create a safe place where seekers can genuinely do their seeking. 'It's not about winning the argument in the small groups,' said Nicky Gumbel. If people have felt that they've had a good time, then they will come back next week. And those questions funnily enough have gone by next week. They may tell you at the end that they didn't get a satisfactory answer to a specific question, but they probably won't raise it again. They seem to have taken on board what was said. They won't admit they're satisfied, but it's all going in. (*Compass* magazine, Spring 2002)

It's always personal

Be aware as you get into discussions in lessons, assemblies and small groups that people rarely speak abstractly. If someone has a question, unless they are a 'red herring merchant' it often comes from a genuine personal experience or situation. For example, I have been asked 'Why does God allow small babies to die?' I have got plenty of theological answers for that, but I soon realised that the people asking are probably talking about their baby brother or sister that died, so it wouldn't really be appropriate to give them a text book Christian answer to that question. To sympathise and say that God understands is a more helpful and measured response. I'd rather win a friend than an argument!

Tough times

> Pupils and staff at a West Yorkshire school are being offered counselling following the sudden death of the Head Boy. John Harding, 17, died last Wednesday evening. His parents 'Andy' and 'Christine' paid tribute to their smashing son. Mr Jones the Head Teacher said that John was a popular, well respected young man who joined the school at 11 and had a bright future before him. Mr Harding said his son had been ill with depression for nine months. (*Yorkshire Evening Post*, 20 April 1999 – names changed)

John's death was a complete shock and came out of the blue for most people in the school. It affected all areas of school life, especially the sixth form, with which I had had a lot of involvement in the five years I had worked at the school. I made sure that I went to the funeral, which was very sad with 200 young people saying goodbye to one of their friends. Because schools are a microcosm of society, most things happen there, including births and deaths. It was a privilege for me to be able to listen to some young people as they asked a lot of questions after the death in the school.

Another sad incident happened once when we came in to do a Rock Solid. We arrived to set up our stuff and all the young people came rushing up to us saying, 'Have you heard about our teacher?' One of their teachers had collapsed in the classroom, never recovered and died later in hospital. We adjusted what we did that day in Rock Solid and spent time praying for the family of the dead teacher. You could have heard a pin drop – the young people were genuinely moved by this popular teacher dying so suddenly.

It occurred to me that if we want to be involved in school, either as a church leader, a schools worker, a governor or anything else, we need to learn to ride the roller-coaster, to be involved in the celebrations and the tragedies of life. You never quite know what is going to happen in a school.

While I was doing the outreach part of my discipleship training with Youth with a Mission (YWAM) in Northern Ireland back in 1993, I was put in charge of the schools work module. We had a whole series of lessons to do in a school. We'd had an excellent week being involved in school life and we met some great people there. Sari, my friend from YWAM, and I had just finished giving a lesson and we left at the end of school with all the rest of the kids. We crossed the footbridge over the dual carriageway and started to make our way to our host's home, when suddenly I heard a noise behind me and saw what I thought was a bag flying up above the bonnet of a car. Something happened inside of me and I suddenly realised that this wasn't a bag, it was a person. I somehow got across the dual carriageway to the other side of the road and made my way to the scene of the accident, without thinking twice.

A young man of 18 was lying there in the road with blood coming from his head. I just stood over him and started praying. He was still alive and people gathered around, until eventually a doctor stopped and then the ambulance arrived. I continued to pray for this young man, while Sari spoke to and comforted the driver of the vehicle, who was hysterical. The 18-year-old had been hit on the dual carriageway at 50 mph. Apparently his friend had called out to him and he had turned round just for a second and hadn't seen the car that was coming straight at him.

Being so close to an accident like that affected my life for several days afterwards and I still remember it vividly now. I didn't know what I was doing or what I was praying about at the time. I suppose that is what they call 'standing in the gap'. I found out a few days later, just before we left Northern Ireland, that he had died. Sari and I had to talk it through with some people before we could get our lives back to normal.

It just happened that we had an assembly at school the next morning as a whole team. We decided to shelve what we'd planned and I talked honestly from the heart about God and how important our relationship with him is. It was one of those times where God was present and we were able to pray for the family of this young man. Every young person in school seemed to listen intently to what we had to say, as many of them had also witnessed the accident. After those two days it felt as if I'd done ten rounds with Mike Tyson – we were exhausted. It brought home to me then, in my first experience of schools work, that what we do has eternal consequences. But it was also a privilege to be involved in the school at such a difficult and scary time for everyone.

If the head teacher invites you to presentation evenings, school plays or the sixth form ball, then go ahead and celebrate with the school, but also let them know that you are around for the difficult times as well. One of the main things to educate children about is the fact that there are ups and downs in life the whole time, and that is part of the excitement and the sadness of life, in and out of school.

When I started as a schools worker I never expected to go to the funeral of a young person in the school where I was working, but God has taught me so much through that experience and it changed my schools work for ever.

22

What Happens if it Goes Wrong?

Pete Gilbert sent me this story:

> While I was being trained in Swindon when I first joined YFC
> I heard the story of a schools worker who was taking a lesson
> along the lines of seeing is believing. Being determined to
> outdo other schools workers using the same illustration, he
> laced a bunch of flowers heavily with tomato ketchup and pro-
> ceeded to devour the lot in front of the class. Unfortunately he
> didn't realise that this is only possible if you eat the coloured
> petals and do not touch the greenery on the flowers, which is
> often poisonous. So with the greenery and the tomato ketchup
> combined he promptly threw up all over the classroom floor,
> at which point in the nervous spasm he also knocked over the
> tomato ketchup bottle which smashed splattering tomato
> ketchup and vomit up the walls, the pupils and the desks.

I certainly hope that wouldn't happen to you! However, the
best schools workers and youth workers in the world will
make mistakes, and it is helpful to think now how you
would handle it.

One fundamental thing is to know who your support is.
Have in your life and your work a specified group of people

to whom you are accountable. It could be your trustees, your church leaders or the boss in the organisation that you work for. Knowing the lines of management and communication would help you if something difficult did arise in school or you were accused of something falsely, which can and does happen. I was once accused of being involved in a 'racist assembly'. A visiting team was talking about their football skills and sharing their faith. A black member of the team was not able to get involved in this as he did not play football. Straight after the assembly I was asked to go and see the deputy head immediately, which I did. The deputy head then spent five or ten minutes explaining to me why they felt that the assembly was racist (because the black person was left out!). I tried to explain that a misunderstanding had taken place and the talk and presentation was in no way racist, and once I had explained this fully and calmly then the matter was resolved.

'A "very helpful" Christian proceeded to pull me apart on my choice of music and my theology of worship.'

What I learnt from this was that we need to understand how to react to things, and also have people in our lives to whom we can refer schools if they are not happy with the things we are saying. Because I am personally accountable to someone in Leeds, I am able to give a name and a phone number if people have a problem with me. Not only does that show that I am professional and accountable in the things that I do, but it is a great mechanism to get rid of people who do not understand where I am coming from. This happened to me after a gig once, when a 'very helpful' Christian proceeded to pull me apart on my choice of music and my theology of worship. I spent a good ten minutes trying to explain my thoughts and how I had come to these decisions about the music that I play, but she just wasn't interested. Eventually, giving her the number of somebody she could ring diffused the situation and I was able to walk away without getting too affected by that 'very helpful' encouragement!

Schools have very clear lines of communication and management which you should utilise as a schools worker. If you have been in a school long enough then maybe there will be senior members of staff, or other Christian members of staff, that would vouch for you and help you in difficult times.

If you have made a mistake then admit it; if you have said something which has been misunderstood or something which has been theologically incorrect, then just confess that you have done that. It will keep your credibility and integrity in the long run. Try to maintain a healthy level of prayer and a sense of humour in times like this, as often things can blow over fairly quickly and it is very easy to think that your whole ministry is going to collapse around your ears when often it is a misunderstanding that can be dealt with simply and effectively. Take advice from people that you trust, and get some training. If you are able to say you have been on a schools workers' or youth workers' training course, or a child protection course, then a lot of issues will not arise or will be diffused. Having these things as a back-up to what you do is so important for maintaining your professionalism and integrity in a school environment.

Just remember things *will* go wrong, and you might assign those times to 'a spiritual attack' or 'personality clashes', but if you feel you have been misrepresented or misunderstood, how you deal with it is the most important thing. It may be helpful to role-play with fellow workers situations which could possibly go wrong and think about how you would deal with them. Then pray together that the situation *won't* happen, or that God will help you if it does!

23
What About Other Faiths?

The prospect of explaining the Christian faith to pupils from other faiths can seem daunting. It can lead to big differences of opinion and heated debate, but it can also be very rewarding. You are often met with a level of interest and understanding not always found in other pupils. Pupils from other faiths can often understand the concept of religion being central to a person's life. It won't surprise them to hear you talk about God being all important, or affecting every area of your life. They will assume that you go to church, and worship and faith are concepts with which they will be familiar. Explaining the Christian faith in this context isn't necessarily any easier and it still requires careful thought and preparation.

What are you seeking to achieve? Many Christians working with pupils from other faiths have the aim of presenting Christianity in a truthful, positive and interesting way. This is often achieved, not only in explaining the details of the Christian faith, but in living a Christian lifestyle and actively demonstrating the difference knowing Jesus makes. At an appropriate time, the pupils will then be able to reflect on what they have heard and make their own decisions.

. . . When presenting the Christian faith look for areas of common interest. You could ask them about the role of holy books in their faith and then go on to explain the importance of the Bible to Christians and how God speaks to you through it. You could discuss religious festivals, places of worship or beliefs about life after death. Although they are unlikely to be mature in their faith, you will discover areas where pupils can understand the points you make, because of their own religious beliefs. (Taken from the 1996 Schools Ministry Network booklet *Support Your Local School*)

I have yet to come across a school which does not have a mixture of different faiths. It is also important to remember that even among pupils of other faiths, there may be different cultural backgrounds within those faiths (i.e. not all Muslims believe the same things regarding appropriate dress, for example). So get to know the pupils a little bit and learn more about their culture. This will help you to understand them better.

Sometimes you will not see people from other faiths as they may be withdrawn from assemblies or RE lessons, but there will be times when you are addressing the whole school. One of my schools has a higher than normal percentage of Jewish pupils. It is helpful for me to know when they are in assembly and when they are not, but I think that my assemblies are appropriate and relevant enough so that Jewish and other faith pupils are able to hear what I am saying and understand something of it without my ever undermining their faith in any way.

A key to working with other faiths is simply to think twice before speaking. Think about the relevance of what you are saying and maybe avoid certain subjects in certain contexts. I would be very happy to deal with life after death, heaven and hell within an RE lesson, but dealing with that in an assembly with a five-minute talk will often leave a lot to be desired and may leave more room for mis-understanding. As you become experienced in working with pupils of other faiths it will become more natural to you and actually quite exciting. A basic knowledge of their faith and a good healthy attitude to your own should remove the necessity to be overly politically correct.

Never be ashamed of the Christian faith. Most Muslims expect Christians to be proud of their faith and can't understand why Christians in Britain seem so embarrassed about the whole thing. Make sure you don't present Christianity as a white European faith, but include examples of Christianity from, particularly, Africa, Asia and the Middle East. Also do you know any Christians from a different cultural background from your own who would be good in schools? (*Generation to Generation: Building Bridges between Churches and Schools* – Fanfare and Scripture Union publication)

24

Evangelism Versus Education

I am grateful to Jon Burns, Director of Evangelism for British Youth for Christ, for his help in co-writing the following material.

Introduction to the debate

Most people who are involved in schools ministry will at some time or other have debated (whether in their own mind or with others) the reason behind what they are doing. Some see themselves as serving their local community by supporting teachers or the wider work in a school environment. Others, perhaps for reasons of background or calling, see themselves as educators. While others, for similar reasons, may feel called to engage in evangelism in a school setting.

The reason behind what we are doing will always define the way we do what we do. Our motivation often causes us to take high ground over those with different motivation and can easily lead to a debate that might not need to take place.

Youth work and education

Those engaged in full-time youth ministry often find themselves working in schools. Local churches and youth work organisations increasingly expect their youth workers to relate to Christian and non-Christian young people in their local schools whether trained teachers or not. Some youth workers may find themselves engaging in various educational activities (assemblies, lessons, classroom support) and sometimes question what they are doing there.

If we define education as a formal or informal process by which knowledge or skills are taught or passed on, then lots of schools work is by nature educational. Presentations and assemblies, whether religious, ethical or moral, will be educative by agenda.

Informal youth work is, by definition, work with young people in non-formal settings. Lunchtime clubs, after-school clubs, etc., are always available for young people by choice or by option. Youth workers engaged in schools work, however, will inevitably question the appropriateness of direct or relational evangelism while in school time or on school premises.

What is evangelism?

Charles Spurgeon defined evangelism as one beggar telling another beggar where to get some bread. There are many more elaborate definitions available: evangelism is basically the process of sharing good news. The on-going debate of 'evangelism versus social action' is perhaps a diversion when behind both there is the desire by word or deed to share something of Christ and his love.

Many people assume that the word evangelism means a

proclamation style perhaps involving 'altar calls'. Most schools workers would agree that rarely, if ever, would that style of evangelism be appropriate. Nevertheless, if the schools worker is invited to take an RE lesson on a subject relating to Christ, they are either intentionally or unintentionally engaging in evangelism.

Appropriate evangelism in a school setting

It is difficult to set hard and fast rules, for what is appropriate in one school may not be appropriate in another. The hundreds of Catholic schools in the country may be more open to direct Christian teaching than state-run schools in multicultural settings. In some private schools, an overtly Christian emphasis is positively encouraged.

Perhaps the firmest rule should be that permission should be sought for any activity or comment that may be misinterpreted. Therefore, the person in charge of an assembly, or the classroom teacher you are working with, needs to be informed and in agreement with what you are about to do or say. Don't always assume that a Christian teacher will be more willing to allow you freedom in an evangelistic sense than a non-Christian. In my own experience, the opposite has often been the case.

There is a safe and acceptable way to say most things. Taking the line, 'As a Christian, I believe . . .' as opposed to 'Obviously it is true that . . .' will save a schools worker hours of apologies and lots of closed doors. Equally, you are always on safer ground answering directly a question that has been asked of you than simply proclaiming your opinions and beliefs. Therefore learn to tell stories, ask questions and always leave time in a classroom for open discussion or private questions afterwards.

In today's multicultural Britain, extra sensitivity must be shown in all schools, but particularly in those in which children from different religious and ethnic backgrounds are represented. Sensitivity will begin with understanding, not so that we can simply win arguments, but so we can show genuine respect. I have a friend who works in a school that is 98 per cent Bangladeshi, but he has found that using stories in assemblies from the book of Genesis will allow him to talk appropriately about God and his character.

The law in England, however, allows that assemblies should be broadly Christian in nature and that religious education, although inclusive of other faiths, has a strong weight towards the Christian story, and we should take confidence from this.

Different needs – different roles

I believe that any approach to a school needs to be with a heart to serve. Therefore in discussions with key teaching or management staff of a school, it is very fair to ask, 'How can I help?' Sometimes that might call for us to play a specific role in a school that would not normally be part of our strategy. For example, a secondary school I was working in had a PE staff shortage for a term; they were able to find internal cover for all except Friday mornings. I was able to provide supply cover for a term simply coaching sport. That act of service totally changed my working relationship with the school. The trust that is established through genuine servanthood opens doors that a hidden agenda never could. The following four years in that school I have never been able to repeat anywhere else.

Therefore it may be appropriate for a season to serve a

school with classroom support, extra supervision for trips or holidays, pre- or post-schooltime clubs, or in a wide variety of other roles.

Different roles – different calling

As in all walks of Christian life and ministry, it is important that we don't take the high ground because of our own specific calling over and above those who have been called to serve Christ differently. I have come across very faithful schools workers who believed that their role was to serve and resource Christian teachers in a given area, others who felt called to establish prayer support networks in the community. Other Christians see God's call in serving schools as governors or as part of PTAs. None of these are more or less important than those who feel called to engage with young people in school settings. Equally, those engaged in pre- or post-exclusion work (i.e. working with young people who are excluded from mainstream school) are of no greater or lesser value than those engaged in the more standard practices of assemblies and lessons. It has been exciting in the last few years to watch the development of more specific ministries within schools with people using arts or sport-based gifts to engage with young people.

Process or crisis?

A hot debate, which affects discussions like this, is whether people come to faith suddenly through a crisis or journey towards faith as a process. I believe that it is both – in different combinations. Lee Jackson personally journeyed towards God but there were significant events in his life

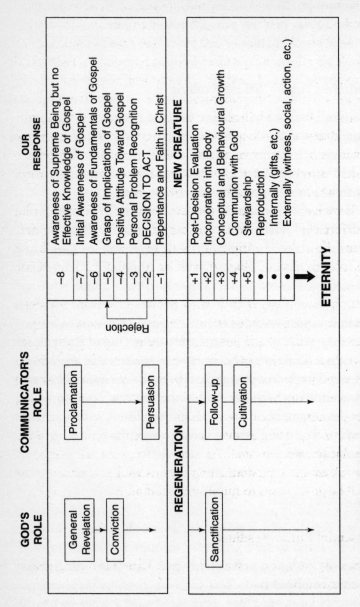

GOD'S ROLE	COMMUNICATOR'S ROLE		OUR RESPONSE
General Revelation	Proclamation	−8	Awareness of Supreme Being but no Effective Knowledge of Gospel
Conviction		−7	Initial Awareness of Gospel
		−6	Awareness of Fundamentals of Gospel
		−5	Grasp of Implications of Gospel
	Persuasion	−4	Positive Attitude Toward Gospel
		−3	Personal Problem Recognition
		−2	DECISION TO ACT
		−1	Repentance and Faith in Christ

Rejection

REGENERATION

		+1	Post-Decision Evaluation
Sanctification	Follow-up	+2	Incorporation into Body
		+3	Conceptual and Behavioural Growth
	Cultivation	+4	Communion with God
		+5	Stewardship
		•	Reproduction
		•	Internally (gifts, etc.)
		•	Externally (witness, social, action, etc.)

NEW CREATURE

ETERNITY

(Taken from www.brigade.org.today/articles/tellitoften.html)

that brought him to decisions of faith, like his confirmation and a Spring Harvest youth meeting in 1985.

The 'Engel's scale' opposite is helpful in this context. The model has been adapted and added to over the years, and depicts the roles of God, the communicator and the listener in the process of communicating the gospel. Everyone we talk to falls somewhere on this scale in terms of their spiritual decision-making process and receptivity to the gospel. There is no 'quality of ministry' scale here! Moving people from −8 to −7 is just as important as moving people from −2 to +5, but maybe a bit less glamorous.

If we have been taught that evangelism is about guerrilla warfare raids into enemy territory, then we will not understand how real relationships and genuine journeys bring people to faith in God, as well as traditional evangelistic events.

I do not believe that Christian schools work needs to be exclusively about education or exclusively about evangelism. For example, if you educate young people about the crucifixion, they may be drawn closer to God as they begin to understand the price Jesus paid for us. Similarly, if you do evangelism in the local community you educate young people about their social responsibilities. I believe that good and responsible evangelism in a school setting will be, by nature, educational. As schools workers serve schools and share the Christian story, they as well as their message will be good news to pupils and staff alike.

Essential further reading:

Sowing, Reaping, Keeping by Laurence Singlehurst (Crossway Books)

25
For Managers and Leaders

Here are a few tips that I wish I'd learnt earlier in my ministry as a schools worker.

1. Learn to manage yourself. Remember that schools work can be draining and exhausting work, always sharing from yourself, your experience, and your walk with God, so it is very important that we keep ourselves fresh. Put whatever you need to have in place, in order to allow yourself to continue doing the job effectively for years to come, instead of a couple of mad years before burn out!

2. I have found it helpful to have a Board of Trustees and a line manager, not only from a work point of view but also as purely pastoral support. He asks me about work but also allows me to speak openly and personally about my life with Clare, family and everything else.

3. Ask yourself whether you should have a team of people who would pray regularly for you and your family. Think about who you know and would trust to pray for you. People who are not related to your job

and not even related to your church may be more helpful and objective. They don't give advice or counsel but just promise to pray and maybe meet you once a term to pray with you.

4. Don't allow your talks to become too technical or theological; remember that God is your dad and being a Christian is an intimate relationship with him, and not an impersonal relationship with a 'spooky god' in the sky.

5. Learn to be thankful for your job and the privilege it is to be able to shape your own work. Yes, we probably aren't paid as much as many other workers, but we have to learn to be thankful and happy with what we have got (or we will go mad!).

6. Don't plan so far ahead that you miss the day-to-day stuff. Suck every ounce of life from time in school, so that you do not just 'wait' for the next week's club or the next big youth event around the corner.

7. Get advisers who can help you with your schools work or your management issues from the real world of work, not just from Christian sources.

8. Keep a clear record of what you do, so that you don't repeat yourself but can look back and be pleased at the opportunities God has given you.

9. If you are a manager, consider using associate workers i.e. workers who are not paid by you, but who do work partly on your behalf. They may be local youth or children's workers.

10. Remember that you are not there to promote yourself but to develop a team for the future and for greater effectiveness.

11. There are some issues that only yourself and the trustees need to talk about as managers or leaders of the

project. However, many things can be shared with workers and volunteers, so try to avoid the culture of secret meetings in corridors and develop a culture of openness instead.

12. Make sure you communicate well with your supporters and your prayer partners. A good newsletter or email is essential to a Christian project; make sure it is well designed, informative and inspirational. If you fail to communicate with your colleagues, volunteers or supporters it will be your downfall. Make sure that people know everything they need to know. The devil is keen to disrupt communications between Christians, so prioritise this as a way of making things run easier and smoother.

Fund-raising

If you are fund-raising for a project, there are no easy ways to do it. It is just hard work! However, the best advice I have had has been from a book called *Avoiding the Waste Paper Basket* by Tim Cook (a London Voluntary Service Council publication). This is an excellent worksheet type book, which gives you straightforward advice about applying to trusts. It also gives you sample letters which are very helpful.

- Always fund-raise simultaneously to your local supporters, churches, trusts and possibly to the business community, as this will give weight to your applications.
- Consider match-funding: will a church match money that a trust will give? This will encourage money to come forward and also show that you are committed and supported well elsewhere.

- Remember when fund-raising, the salary for a worker is not the only cost involved in employing somebody. Consider expenses, National Insurance, administration and management costs (i.e. your time).

- Be aware that some schools (if they know you well enough) may actually have some money that they could release to you for the work you do for them. It is sometimes possible to get money for a specific series of lessons or projects in school. Use this with care, and ask advice if you are in any doubt, as this could damage your relationship with a school very quickly!

- Before attempting any significant fund-raising, it is important that you sit down and ask yourself as many questions as you can about your organisation. Imagine people asking the most difficult questions, write these down and find a way to answer them or to alleviate your weaknesses. This is a priceless exercise when embarking on fund-raising. It is important that you know your organisation, vision, aims and strengths back to front and inside out. It may also be helpful to have a presentation on Powerpoint or OHP that other people or workers could use on your behalf.

Employing staff

There has been a lot of speculation and misinformation about the European equal treatment directive; this outlaws discrimination in employment and vocational training on the grounds of age, sex and religion. Faithworks are campaigning about this. Keep in contact with Faithworks and you will be able to find out the latest development on this new directive. The 'Keep the Faith' campaign urges government to think again and allow faith-based organisations to be free to employ those who share that faith. See Appendix 2 at the back of this book.

Finally, why not consider doing a management course tailored to you? I did the Management Development training programme run by the Directory of Social Change. It was one day a month for ten months and credits were available by completing a portfolio and two extra days' revision. It was an excellent course and helped me meet and learn from other local voluntary sector managers. The DSC can be contacted on 0151 7080117.

26

Real Stories

The following are true stories from school and youth workers across the country received via Schools Ministry Network.

Tanked up

We were doing a practical demonstration of baptism to a Year 7 class, involving a teddy bear and a fish tank. Unfortunately the tank was too heavy to carry up two floors with water in, so we had to carry it up empty. Once there we couldn't figure out how to fill it up. The caretaker came to the rescue with the fire hose. The kids enjoyed it; the bear got wet and the caretaker thought we were all completely bonkers! And we had to empty the tank out of the window!

Changed life

A young girl I knew from a single parent family on a council estate was always in trouble at school for her behaviour. Yet she had such a life-changing experience of God at school that when she left at 16 she went and spent a year doing mission work with Jackie Pullinger in the walled city in Hong Kong.

Cupboard love

One night at the youth group we showed Steve Chalke's 'Lessons in Love' video. To add to the atmosphere we turned the lights out. During the night a parent walked in, saw we were watching TV and promptly walked out again. No one could concentrate for the rest of the session because, instead of going out of the door, the parent had mistaken the exit and walked into the cupboard! Obviously too embarrassed to come out again, they had spent the next 20 minutes standing in the broom cupboard with the light off. We had to send everyone out of the room before the said parent could be coaxed out again. (Mark)

He's got Jesus!

A non-Christian head teacher said to the teacher who runs the Scripture Union group in primary school, 'David's got Jesus! He can't stop talking about it and he's reading his Bible.' David is a boy with serious behavioural problems. You would never have guessed in the SU group, except that he answers quiz questions better than anybody else. (Jane)

Tug of war!

During an assembly at a middle school, I was using a rope to illustrate how we need to work together. On one end I had a Year 5 girl and on the other end the tallest teacher in the school – about 6' 6". The teacher won easily. I then asked for some of the girl's friends to help her and about five or six volunteered. As they pulled on the rope, it suddenly snapped and the teacher flew backwards onto the floor, while the children landed in a heap at the other end! The whole school broke into uproar, and when I followed up with a reading from Ecclesiastes 4 it took on a whole new meaning! ('Two are better than one, if one falls down the other can help him up and a rope of three cords is not easily broken.')

'Jules Holland!'

About seven years ago I was in a school assembly with someone from my church. We were doing 'Forgiveness: the parable of the unmerciful servant'. There was a bit of banter between us about how many times we should forgive each other, etc. Then it was time for the serious bit. Jules went off stage and I started to talk, when he sat down on the piano stool and crash! It smashed! They could all hear, everyone laughed and the 'serious bit' was lost. The best bit was as soon as he did it he came back on stage and said, 'Wayne will you forgive me?' And that just made it. The impromptu nature of schools' work! Weeks later I was back and the girls asked after him . . . now known as the piano stool wrecker! (Wayne)

Tied up!

I once did an assembly in front of a whole school on 'Seeing is Believing', where I cut a teacher's tie off with a pair of scissors just below the knot. Naturally the teacher had been carefully prepared in advance and provided with an old tie from an Oxfam shop, but unfortunately my colleague had passed the tie to the wrong teacher and I cut his 'real' tie off!

Watch your words!

At the end of a hard-working schools week a colleague and I ran a Friday evening concert, with an opportunity for response, in the local church that we had trained up previously and linked to the school. It was a difficult evening with a small element of disruptive lads, and our intercessors in the prayer room were asking God for an atmosphere of peace and conviction! When it came to the moment of the gospel, as is so often the case an incredible godly silence fell upon the place and the disruptive lads in the front row listened for the first time that evening. Upon which my colleague turned to them in the middle of his preaching and addressing them said, 'And even now as you are listening to me the Holy Spirit is prompting your consciences and right now you lads on the front row are feeling little pricks . . . little pricks of conscience!' By which time we had totally lost the evening and that was that!

I bumped into the head teacher

The head teacher was walking to her car when a pupil ran around the corner and bumped into her, knocking her glasses off her face and onto the tarmac. She knelt down to pick up her glasses without realising they had fallen into the path of my moving van. Just after I saw her lunge in front of my van I heard a bump! I had knocked over the head teacher on my way out of school after doing a lesson for Jesus! Fortunately, she brushed herself off and went on her way, glad that her glasses were not broken! I was just relieved that I hadn't killed anyone!

I'll explain it again!

I remember the remarkable experience of preaching the gospel off the back of escapology in one of the best known public schools in the country. At the end of the evening and with the full permission of the staff I made an appeal with an opportunity for response to the gospel, at which point about two-thirds of the 200 or so boys voluntarily attending stood to their feet. I sat them all down again, went through the gospel again, making it even punchier and harder in its demands on lifestyle and discipling and repeated the appeal only to find that two-thirds responded again. The English teacher involved was swamped with responses, and a Christian Union was set up which continued to influence the school with the gospel for some years following. (Pete)

Real quotes collected by LFIS

'Before I came here tonight I decided to check what you actually did, so I asked my two granddaughters (Years 7 and 9) if they had heard of you, and they both know who you are. So in my eyes that's success if the kids know who you are!' (Woman at church PCC meeting)

'I loved the holidays but was sad on Wednesday because it meant I couldn't come to Rock Solid.' (Kid at Rock Solid)

'I don't know what you do with the kids, but keep doing it because they always come back to lessons really happy!' (Teacher)

'It's not like asking just anyone to do an assembly, because you are part of the school.' (Teacher)

'What you've been doing is amazing!' (PE teacher)

'We don't just welcome you as visitors but as friends now.' (Teacher)

'You've been amazing – can you come in full time?' (PE teacher)

Add yours here . . .

27

To Make You Think

Here are some thoughts to get you going . . . or keep you going!

- Know your discipline structure and keep to it!
- No low-cut tops (girl to girl advice).
- Just before you go into school, check your flies and check for bogies!
- Learning mentors are good people to get to know.
- Leave plenty of time to get to school – there is always an unexpected delay to slow the traffic.
- Leave the room as you found it.
- Don't take yourself too seriously.
- Hold it all lightly.
- Don't use gaffer tape on the floor; masking tape comes off easily.
- Learn to spell chlamydia and gonorrhoea.
- Have a couple of games you can pull out of the bag at a moment's notice! (See Appendix 4 for details.)
- Write *everything* in your diary.
- Get good prayer support.
- Get a good filing system.

- Make a record of everything you do and how it went.
- Share resources.
- Quality not quantity.
- Be yourself: don't make things up; tell real stories from your life; kids will listen and know when you are being authentic.
- Don't copy other people's style – find your own.
- Use what you are good at to serve the school. (I still haven't found a way to use synchronised swimming!)
- Make connections with the churches local to the school, for as many ways of support as possible i.e. prayer, volunteers, money. Try to get opportunities to speak at the churches about what you are doing.
- Make sure the teacher writes down when you are coming in so they don't forget.
- There is more to schools work than mainstream schools. Have you considered contacting any local special schools in your area – those that deal with people with disabilities or behavioural difficulties? Is there a young persons' secure unit near to you? How about a project working with excluded pupils or those at risk of exclusion? These are more specialised areas, but in my experience of special schools and exclusion units they are also desperately in need of help and Christian input.
- I once used a walking stick (for the long walk into the hall with the head teacher) pretending I had a broken leg. I talked about the myths people had about God and then with a dramatic movement dropped my walking stick and emphasised the fact that often we make the wrong assumptions about others and God. It was dramatic, but I think the head teacher felt a bit cheated by the stunt! I don't recommend stunts, unless they are carefully thought through. (Bounce the idea off local

ministers, teachers or others with experience who speak in schools.)

- As kids come into the class, sit in a relaxed manner on the front desk and engage them in conversation where they are telling you more about what they know than you are telling them what you know, thus earning the right later of sharing the gospel with them. Use the first few minutes of the school lesson to introduce the lesson rules (e.g. lots of fun, visiting guest teacher, when I speak you listen and when you speak with your hand in the air I listen, etc.).

- Eye contact, tone of voice, pace, body language are all vital elements, not only of control but also of communication.

- As long as you tag every statement you make with the phrase 'I believe', you can get away with an awful lot of content.

- Don't take your diary into school; take suggested dates and call back. That way you stay in better control of your diary and can pace yourself more!

- Even if it goes very wrong indeed, you must try and leave in the best way that you can on good terms thus keeping the door open for the future.

- Err on the side of caution and ask the school what they expect you to wear. Gradually you may be able to become more casual as they get to know you.

- I have a lot of respect for the phenomenal success of Alpha. However, in my experience, it doesn't really answer the questions that youth are asking. For example, when a young person was asked in a session, 'Why did Jesus die?' the answer they gave was, 'Because he stopped breathing!' Know your young people and what is relevant to them.

- Ask God to show you his heart for the young people in

the school that you are trying to reach. If you haven't cried for the young people that you are working with then you haven't captured God's heart, and if you don't cry then you need to learn how to.

- Remember that school life as a schools worker is fragile; treat it with care and respect at all times, as it is easy to destroy something good very quickly.

- Why not go to some quizzes and parent–teacher evenings and even get invited to staff parties? It's always good for a laugh, going out for a meal with the staff.

- Be aware that receptionists, secretaries, caretakers and other support staff can be the key to your success in the school. Give them lots of chocolate and try to become their friends. It will be worth it!

- A full life is not necessarily fulfilling; use your time carefully.

- Use current events to get a point across.

- An important lesson for young people today is Galatians chapter 6 verses 7 and 8 – 'you will reap what you sow' (or as they say 'what goes around comes around!').

- Put Jesus at the centre of everything.

- Take people with you, so that after you have moved on, things will continue.

- Don't make your appointments in school so tight time-wise that you don't have time to be there early and to hang about afterwards.

- Find people that inspire you and spend some time with them.

- Do not pretend to be perfect but admit some of your failings and weaknesses (sensitively).

- Always make your talks practical. What can they do because of the talk you have just given? What can they do this week?

- God uses people who are not Christians.
- Look for similarities between you and other Christians, and not differences.
- Find the balance between being radical and being relevant.
- Remember that not all activities with young people are classed as youth work. A lesson or an assembly is something they must attend, but a lunchtime or after school activity is voluntary. This is the key to youth work. If they volunteer to be with you, that's when the relationship changes and true youth work can begin and depth is brought to your relationships with young people. (I would count informal conversations with young people, before or after a compulsory activity, as true youth work – neglect those times at your peril.)

'I say to UK youth workers, "Don't be too enamoured at the so-called success of big American youth ministries." Many of them are a mile wide and an inch deep.' (Tony Jones, Colonial Church of Edina, Minnesota.)

Empowerment

During the 80s and 90s this word 'empowerment' became the cornerstone of most youth workers' training. It is still especially popular among local authority youth workers, as most of their training is based around this idea.

Empowerment can be a complicated and sociological thing, but in my experience the best way to consider any youth or schools work that you are doing is to

- make sure you don't do everything yourself
- take the young people with you

- get them to help you
- allow them to make mistakes in a controlled environment so that you can empower them to become the best they can.

It is very easy as a schools worker to put on a 'good show', do everything yourself and leave the kids with a nice bit of entertainment but feeling quite powerless. Encourage them to help you in things that you do. For instance, in lunchtime groups I would often ask young people to help us to set up or to pack the stuff away. Allow the young people to do some of the practical things that are involved in the groups, like playing the music or giving out pens and paper. If their confidence grows, you could let them speak up front or lead a small group.

What are you going to leave behind?

Somebody once said that the mark of a good leader is not what they do, but what they leave behind them. Imagine yourself leaving the school. What would you leave behind, and what would the young people do if you weren't there, especially the Christian young people? Have you helped to develop their skills to continue God's work in the school, or have you maintained a relationship of 'I am the provider and you are the receiver'? Is it busyness that prevents us from empowering young people?

'Education is what survives when what has been learned has been forgotten.' (B.F. Skinner, American Psychologist, *New Scientist*, May 1964)

For further thinking

- If you are travelling backwards and forwards, have you considered living near the schools that you work in?
- Some youth workers deliberately go and shop in the areas that they work in, even if they don't live there, just so that they will see the faces and get the flavour of the community and meet the young people around the place. That is part of true holistic schools work.
- There are three main types of youth work. There's attached youth work; there is detached youth work; does that mean that schools work is semi-detached youth work?
- Do you equip the young people that you work with to live well or just to get into heaven?
- What is church? Know that you are the church – just don't tell anyone!
- To what extent is our purpose in youth work to entertain?
- Is the work that is done in secret the most important?
- Christians seem to panic about future legislation and whether or not it would exclude Christians from working in schools. I firmly believe that if we have good relationships with the schools then the legislation in many ways will not matter, because we will find opportunities to work and the staff will trust us to work appropriately.
- You are responsible for your own motivation.

Resources

Organisations/website addresses

ACET (Aids Care Education & Training) provide training for sexual health and relationship-based issues from a practical Christian worldview: www.acetuk.org

AMAZE is an association of Christian children's and youth workers. It is the first of its kind in this country and has been a great help to both full-time and part-time workers and managers in youth and children's work, promoting professionalism and good practice. They do the excellent AMAZE manual, which is a complete guide including practical examples of how to employ and advertise for children's, youth and schools workers: www.amaze.org.uk

Care for Education: www.care.org.uk/dept/education

CaSS (Christians and Sheffield Schools) have some very concise and helpful leaflets produced as guidelines for good practice for youth workers, schools and schools workers. Contact linda@cass-su.org.uk

CRED – Christian Relief Education and Development: www.cred.org.uk

The Evangelical Alliance is especially interested in the issue of faith schools at the moment and has a very large library and database of materials: www.eauk.org

HOPE UK is a Christian charity which deals with drugs and alcohol issues: www.hopeuk.org

Leeds Youth Cells Network is a network of youth cells in and around Leeds, who are working across denominational boundaries: www.leedsyouthcells. co.uk

Oasis Trust provide excellent youth worker training and youth resources: www.oasistrust.org

Schools Ministry Network – See Appendix 2 for details.

Scripture Union – the original schools workers. Lots of resources and help in the education field at www.scriptu-reunion.org.uk

Soul Survivor – youth events and festivals with a heart for worship: www.soulsurvivor.com

The Stapleford Centre gives advice, help and training to teachers and people on school related matters: www.stapleford-centre.org

2turntables.co.uk is a network of Christian DJs who can do workshops with young people as well as gigs and training.

Youth For Christ (YFC) is an excellent and growing resource of touring bands, year-out people, sports (fly and kick) and community action teams and helpful resources for schools work. They also developed the Rock Solid programme. You can check them out at www.YFC.co.uk

Youth Specialties is an American publishing company which has some excellent resources which YFC now import into this country. They do great talks and games books: www.youthspecialties.com

Youthwork magazine keeps you up to date with current trends and resources that are available for youth workers. The website is especially helpful at www.youthwork.co.uk

Other websites worth visiting

ACT (Association of Christian Teachers): www.christianteachers.org

Christians in Sport: www.christiansinsport.org.uk

Christian Research Association (for all those facts and figures you keep hearing!): www.christian-research.org.uk

www.crusaders.org.uk – the general Crusader website with lots of links.

www.damaris.org – the best culture-watching Christian website around – a must!

www.life2themax.net – an amazing website covering sex, drugs and other youth-related topics.

www.olivetree.com – get a free or cheap Bible for your palm- or pocket-PC.

www.presidentforaday.org – an excellent CDRom on world issues is available from this site for school use.

www.relessonsonline.com – it does exactly what it says on the tin!

www.vizaviz.org – schools work organisation which provides quality videos for youth work.

This is by no means an exhaustive list. These are just some of the organisations that I have used or come across in the last few years or so, and I'm sure you can add your own.

Books

A lot of these books and resources are commented on at the Leeds Faith In Schools website – www.LFIS.org with suggestions on how to use them. It is continually updated.

50 Life-Lifting Devotions for Youth Workers by Herbert Brokering and Scott C. Noon (Canube Books).

A Really Great Assembly by Graham Knox and Chris Chesterton (YFC and Scripture Union).

Accompanying by Maxine Green and Chandu Christian (Church House Publishing).

Avoiding the Wastepaper Basket, a practical guide to applying to grant-making trusts by Tim Cook (London Voluntary Service Council publication).

Awakening Cry by Pete Greig (Novto Publishing) available from www.24-7prayer.com.

Basketball Skills and Drills by Gerry V. Kraus, edited by Howard Garfinkel (available from Sportserve 01943 603669).

Big Questions by Steve Legg (Christian Publicity Organisation Publication).

Children of Revival by Van Lane (Revival Press).

Dead Men Walking by Lee Jackson and Baz Gascoigne (Kingsway).

Freedom Ride by Alyn Haskey (Marshall Pickering).

Future Wise by Dr Patrick Dixon (HarperCollins).

Generation-to-Generation (Building Bridges Between Churches and Schools) (Scripture Union).

Gutter Feelings by Pip Wilson (Marshall Pickering).

Issues Facing Christians Today by John Stott (Marshall Pickering).

It Makes Sense by Stephen Gaukroger (Scripture Union).

It's Your Move! (Scripture Union).

Just Think about That (40 outlines for secondary assemblies) compiled by Phil Wason (Scripture Union).

Key Christian Beliefs by Chris Wright (Lion Publishing).

New Celts by Roger Ellis and Chris Seaton (Kingsway).

Ready-made Assemblies About Famous People by Tony Dobinson (Scripture Union).

Running Christian Groups in Secondary Schools by Simon Barker and Bruce Lockard (Scripture Union).

School Assemblies Need You by Richard Dyter (Monarch Publishing).

Schools Work Handbook by Emlyn Williams (Scripture Union).

Sharing the Truth in Love by Ajith Fernando (Discovery House publishers).

Sowing, Reaping, Keeping by Lawrence Singlehurst (Crossway Books). A must-read for all Christians.

Sowing Seeds for Revival by Martin Scott (Sovereign World).

Support Your Local School by Schools Ministry Network (available directly from them).

The Jesus I Never Knew by Philip Yancey (Zondervan).

The Oxford Dictionary of 20th Century Quotations.

The Teenage Boy's Survival Handbook by Nick Harding (Kevin Mayhew Publishing).

The Tide is Running Out (What the English Church Attendance Survey Reveals) by Dr Peter Brierley (Christian Research).

Understanding Leadership by Tom Marshall (Sovereign World).

Understanding Teenagers by Pete Gilbert (Crossway Books).

Was Jesus a Moderate by Tony Campolo (W Publishing).

What is the point of Christmas by J. John (Lion Publishing).

Wigglesworth – The Man Who Walked with God by George Stormont (Harrison House).

Wild at Heart by John Eldridge (Thomas Nelson Publishing).

Your local Agreed Syllabus for Religious Education should be available from the school or LEA if you need to get it.

Videos

A View From the Terraces: Excellent for use in schools. (Delirious' first video: Furious Records).

DC Talk: Good clips of DC Talk in concert, live gig and stage dive (Alliance Media).

Encounters with Angels: Christians talk about experiencing real angels and how they change their lives. (Mark-it Television 1997).

How to Train Your Parents: Rock Solid promo video (Youth For Christ).

Illegal Access: Heaven and hell (Tear Fund).

Jesus (1999 television mini series): The best yet film about Jesus. Not available in this country yet. (US – Trimark home video).

Lagos 2000: 1 million plus people in a church service! (CFAN).

Make Love Last: Very funny video about sex (CARE).

Manifesto: Steve Chalke on the Third World (Oasis).

More Than Champions: Famous Christians talking about their life in sport (Christians in Sport).

Red Zebra: Tear Fund resource on global issues.

Serious Prayer: Prayer ideas and teaching on prayer (SU).

Transformations 1 and 2: How God has transformed communities and villages (Sentinel Group).

The 24/7 vision: (www.24-7prayer.com).

Feature Films

All Quiet on the Western Front: Very harrowing film on war/lessons on war.

Apollo 13: Good clips about 'will we make it?' What do you believe?

As Good As It Gets: Excellent film about rudeness and not being politically correct. Use with care!

Billy Elliot: A boy from a working-class background tries to become a dancer. Use with editing and care.

Blast From the Past Story: An innocent person being different in an experienced world.

Braveheart: Use with care. Excellent about faith and passion.

City of Angels: Lessons on angels.

Cool Runnings: Good clip at the end about determination and perseverance.

Dead Poet's Society: three or four clips to be used on changing the way you look at things and standing up for what you believe in.

Death Becomes Her: Do you want to be immortal?

Fantastic Voyage: Journey inside the body; good for HIV lessons.

Fifth Element: Film about a saviour / Messiah narrative.

Forrest Gump: Excellent on bullying/friendship, etc.

Galaxy Quest: Spoof sci-fi with good clips about pretending to be who you're not.

Gladiator: Great clips about working as a team with passion, but power corrupts.

Good Morning Vietnam: War.

Grease: Classic clips about peer pressure.

Independence Day: Clip at end of film about someone giving their life for others.

Indiana Jones and the Last Crusade

Jerry Maguire: About breaking the mould and making a difference, having purpose.

Jesus Christ Superstar: Looking at Jesus from a different angle.

Jesus of Nazareth: Good crucifixion scene but a bit miserable all round! DVD.

Kevin and Perry Go Large

Leap of Faith: About fake religion and false Christianity.

Liar Liar: About lying.

Michael: Film about an angel.

Miracle Maker: Excellent animated story of Jesus.

Monty Python and the Holy Grail: Irreverent, but very funny, look at religion.

Mr Holland's Opus: About teaching young people.

Never Been Kissed: About 'fitting in' and peer pressure.

Oliver: Classic clips about poverty.

Parenthood: Life's ups and downs.

Patch Adams: Great clips regarding making a difference in people's lives/being different.

Philadelphia: For use in HIV lessons re AIDS prejudice.

Pleasantville: Film about 'sin'.

Pretty Woman: How you treat people, plus beauty/pressure.

Prince of Egypt: Classic animated film about Moses (not strictly true to biblical account).

Robin Hood – Prince of Thieves

Roxanne: What people look like/beauty.

Saving Private Ryan: Harrowing tale of heroism and war.

Schindler's List: Heroic tale of Jewish lives saved from the Holocaust.

Shadowlands: Film about suffering and death.

She's All That: How we view people, and peer pressure.

Sister Act: Lots of classic clips about going into the community.

Small Screen Big Picture: Great short clips about poverty. Edit for use in groups.

Speed: Pressure/ stress.

The Apostle: Film about finding and losing faith.

The Blues Brothers: Great scene in the church and about getting a vision from God to do something.

The Bodyguard: Classic scene where someone gives their life for someone else.

The Fugitive: 'Leap of Faith' clip.

The Mask: Comedy about masks/dreaming about being different.

The Patriot: Fight for what you believe.

Titanic: Death, letting go, finding your passion, living life to the full.

Toy Story 2: Excellent clip about things not being as they seem (first part).

Waking Ned: Would you lie to get £1million?

Wall Street: Greed.

Television

Bart Wars (The Simpsons).

Blackadder Goes Forth, Series 4: The bit where they go 'over the top' is very moving.

Christmas You've Been Framed

Kevin's Guide 2 Being A Teenager: For use in youth workers' training.

Kilroy: 'I Was Bullied': Talk show about bullying.

Mr Bean: Merry Mishaps: Christmas.

Mr Bean: Perilous Pursuits: Church sketch.

The Fast Show: Christian policeman sketch.

The Royle Family: Great Christmas clips.

Son of God: Showing the possible face of Jesus.

Star Trek: The Next Generation: Episode 32 'Why are we here?'

The Best of Jerry Springer: Use with care! Excellent clips of people who have messed up their lives.

The Best of The Simpsons: There's always stuff to use from the Simpsons!

The Simpsons: Heaven and Hell: Bart sells his soul, and 'Homer the Heretic'.

The Truman Show: Is there anyone out there?

The Very Best of Father Ted: Great clips about how ridiculous religion is.

Ultimate Ride: On board cameras on roller coasters etc.

There are more books and videos at the website www.LFIS.org (click on resources), with comments and ways to use them to aid your planning. Happy hunting!

Faithworks Campaign Objectives

Firstly, the aim of Faithworks is to empower and inspire every local Church to rediscover its role at the heart of community. This will concentrate on the provision of resources and services to allow churches and other local faith-based organisations to engage in projects in their local communities. It will give these, often small, projects a national voice and representation at the highest level.

Secondly, Faithworks will challenge and change the public perception of the Church by engaging both media and government. This objective seeks to continue the work of the Faithworks Campaign prior to the June 2001 election, by ensuring that local church and other faith-based community projects are accurately represented in the media and have a high priority in the setting of local and national policy.

Thirdly, Faithworks will promote Christian values within our society

www.faithworks.info

Kids Klub Leeds

Kidz Klub Leeds is a non-denominational children's church, which meets every Saturday morning in Bridge Street Church in Leeds. It is supported mainly by six churches in Leeds across the denominations, who visit the kids in their localities every week. The kids are bussed in from their areas to the central location where they have a 'mad' time learning about God and other exciting things. It is well run and great fun. Frontline church in Liverpool had the first UK Kidz Klub, which was originally an idea from Bill Wilson in New York who regularly has 20,000+ kids. It is one of the most effective outreaches I have ever seen and reaches people who have no, or very little contact, with any churches. I am helping find ways to connect the kids that are too old for Kidz Klub into youth cells and groups around Leeds, which in itself is a great challenge.

www.kidzklubleeds.org.uk

Schools Ministry Network Objectives

Schools Ministry Network is a voluntary association of Christian organisations and individuals working with schools. In joining the Network, members commit themselves to its objectives, principles and practice. Membership does not imply that any individual has undergone any particular training or is accredited in any way. Members are ultimately responsible to their own employers or organisations.

The objectives of the Network are:

1. To promote integrity of Christian ministry in schools and appropriate standards of practice
2. To co-operate for strategic planning and placement of people and resources
3. To share resources and ideas, provide credibility, and give opportunities for fellowship and training
4. To encourage a wider involvement of Christian churches and organisations in ministry in schools

Principles and practice:

1. We recognise schools to be places of education and seek to work with them in appropriate ways

2. We believe Christians have a responsibility to make a positive contribution to the whole school community

3. We seek to assist pupils to evaluate Christianity as a way of life, by, for example:
   i) helping them understand the basic Christian beliefs
   ii) sharing the relevance of Christianity to different areas of life
   iii) assisting pupils in forming and/or clarifying personal values
   iv) supporting on-going Christian work in schools
   v) giving pupils a positive experience of meeting Christians
   vi) bringing personal and professional support for Christian teachers

4. We recognise the importance of a strategic, long-term approach and ministry in the school community

5. We seek to work in conjunction with, and mindful of, the school staff and not in isolation

6. We seek to co-operate with other Christians in the school community

7. We seek to identify and make contact with Christians already working in a school before beginning something new

8. We show respect for school administration, staff and parents, and never knowingly undermine them

9. We seek to teach Christian principles, while not promoting denominations

10. We are united in purpose yet affirm our diversity in approach and style, within the parameters of the above

APPENDIX 3

Three Assembly Ideas

Rock Solid assembly for Year 7

OK, we are going to play a game. There will be a prize for the first person who answers this question correctly. Put your hands up to guess. 'What am I?'

- Homer Simpson is crazy about me
- I am sweet
- I am round
- I have a hole
- I am covered in sugar
- You can eat me

(Obviously the answer is a doughnut.)

Then play the Doughnut Dangle game as described in Appendix 4.

Talk

The doughnut has a hole in it. You might be thinking it's Year 7, it's lunchtime, what am I going to do at lunchtime? Maybe your lunchtime will have a hole in it; it will be boring, empty and you're not really sure what to do, so how can you make your lunchtime more like a jam doughnut full of excitement? Well . . . Rock Solid is a lunchtime club, every Friday lunchtime in Mr Haskins' drama studio. We play mad and crazy games, we have chocolate for

203

prizes, we chat, we discuss stuff that goes on at school, at home, we have music, we chill out, have fun and we hang out and get to know each other better.

Why do we call it Rock Solid? Well, if you think about it, what kinds of things are important to us in life, what do we aim for, what do we need to survive and what do we like to have in our lives? Things will be said like fame, good health, money, possessions, good family, good social life and maybe even God.

All of these things are here today and could unfortunately be gone tomorrow. Obviously you know people can lose their jobs, you can't be famous for ever and bad things can happen even to members of our families, but the one person who never goes away, never changes, the one person who is Rock Solid in our lives is God. God never goes and God loves us no matter what we do.

That is what Rock Solid is all about. Come and get to know more, make new friends and have some fun with us Friday lunchtime – see you there! Get a flyer from us at the end if you are interested in knowing more.

Self-worth (Shrek) assembly for Years 6–9   13 going on 3C

I introduce myself and the team and get three volunteers to play *The Price Is Right*. Explain this is an old game show that used to be on television a few years ago.

'We are going to show you now products from the latest Argos catalogue and you are going to have to see whether you can guess the right price. Let's play *The Price is Right*.' (This can be done using Powerpoint and a lap top, or you can just do it with big pieces of card.)

Choose three people, give them three cards each and they have to write down the price with a marker pen once you have shown them the pictures of the items. The closest one wins chocolate.

Talk 1

We often value things on the way that they look and judge how much they are worth. This is true of people and not just things. We decide how valuable people are by how pretty they are, or how cool they look, what kind of clothes they are wearing, and so on. Sometimes we forget to take a deeper look at the person inside.

Video clip

We are going to show you a clip from one of our favourite films. This is a clip from *Shrek*. (Use the clip at the end of the film when the Princess Fiona turns into an Ogre.)

Talk 2

Princess Fiona couldn't understand why she stayed as an Ogre. But the fact is that Shrek now knew the real Princess Fiona, and he'd fallen in love with her anyway, so no matter which way the spell had gone, in his eyes she was always beautiful and would remain so.

This reminds us that God says in Isaiah 43, which is in the Old Testament, 'You are precious and honoured in my sight and I love you.' And that is God speaking to us. I think it is a great thing to remember, especially if we feel a bit low because people around us are not very kind about our appearance.

Maybe we could stop and remember that God thinks we are all great and he loves us no matter what we look like, what we wear or even what we do. That's why he says, 'You are precious and honoured in my sight and I love you.'

Thanks for listening.

Gunge (Easter) assembly for Year 6

Introduce the team.

A team member shows a 50p piece and asks, 'What would you do with it? What would you be prepared to do for it? One hundred press ups? Sing a song in front of the assembly?'

A team member gets 50p and puts it in the gunge, and asks, 'Would you put your hand in here?'

Get two volunteers to try to get the 50p out of the gunge.

Talk

We all get in a bit of a mess sometimes don't we? We might do stuff like tell lies, take something that doesn't belong to us, call people names . . . life feels a bit messy and gungy, just like our gunge, doesn't it?

But there is help. God wants to help us to not do that stuff, because he loves us. If you look at the tub of gunge, the tub is the world, the yucky stuff is the bad things that people do, the mess in the world like fighting, people not looking after each other or the environment. And the 50p is each of us. This gunge will affect us all; I know it affects me sometimes.

That's why Jesus came into the world, to help us get out of the mess and to help us to make a difference in the world. He gave us a chance to live our life gunge free.

Conclude by reading a part of the Easter story, or use a suitable song or video clip and explain further if time allows.

Three Best Games!

1. 'Would you rather' is the game where you split a class or a group into two sections left and right and you ask them the question, 'Would you rather?'

   'If you would rather have curry, move to this side of the room; if you would rather have Chinese food, move to the other side of the room.'

   You get used to adding your own fun bits and because of the nature of the game you can gradually bring in life issues and Christianity into the 'would you rather' questions.

   Very flexible, it gets the kids involved because they move around, and the game can be used for many topics.

2. The second best game is 'On the bank, in the river', used by some PE teachers and youth clubs many years ago. You draw a line with tape on the floor (use masking tape as it won't damage the floor). One of the sides is the bank and the other side is the river. Everyone is on the bank to start with and you shout 'bank' 'river' 'river' 'bank', 'river', 'river' etc., as the kids have to jump from one side to the other at the appropriate time and you try and catch them out by doing it faster and tricking them and so on. It's a great knock out game and the young

people seem to love it no matter what age they are. With a roll of masking tape being the only equipment required, it is really handy.

3. Get five volunteers who like to eat doughnuts and five volunteers to feed the people who want doughnuts, and play the doughnut dangle game! Five of the volunteers lie on the floor, face up with arms by their sides; the other five have to feed their partners the doughnut on a string. First pair to finish the doughnut win a prize. You've guessed it – more doughnuts! Make sure everyone gets a round of applause and send them back to their seats.

The 24–7 Vision

www.24-7prayer.com is in my opinion the most exciting website and youth-related movement around. They do mission trips as well as what they call boiler rooms, which are like twenty-first-century monasteries where there is prayer and feeding of the poor. The following is attributed to Pete Greig and used with permission.

The vision is JESUS – obsessively, dangerously, undeniably Jesus.
The vision is an army of young people.
You see bones? I see an army.
And they are FREE from materialism.
They laugh at 9–5 little prisons.
They could eat caviar on Monday and crusts on Tuesday. They wouldn't even notice.
They know the meaning of the Matrix, the way the west was won.
They are mobile like the wind, they belong to the nations. They need no passport. People write their addresses in pencil and wonder at their strange existence.
They are free yet they are slaves of the hurting and dirty and dying.
What is the vision ?
The vision is holiness that hurts the eyes. It makes children

laugh and adults angry. It gave up the game of minimum integrity long ago to reach for the stars. It scorns the good and strains for the best. It is dangerously pure.

Light flickers from every secret motive, every private conversation.

It loves people away from their suicide leaps, their Satan games.

This is an army that will lay down its life for the cause.

A million times a day its soldiers choose to loose

that they might one day win

the great 'Well done' of faithful sons and daughters.

Such heroes are as radical on Monday morning as Sunday night. They don't need fame from names.

Instead they grin quietly upwards and hear the crowds chanting again and again: "COME ON!"

And this is the sound of the underground

The whisper of history in the making

Foundations shaking

Revolutionaries dreaming once again

Mystery is scheming in whispers

Conspiracy is breathing . . .

This is the sound of the underground

And the army is discipl(in)ed.

Young people who beat their bodies into submission.

Every soldier would take a bullet for his comrade at arms.

The tattoo on their back boasts "for me to live is Christ and to die is gain".

Sacrifice fuels the fire of victory in their upward eyes. Winners. Martyrs. Who can stop them?

Can hormones hold them back?

Can failure succeed? Can fear scare them or death kill them?

And the generation prays
like a dying man
with groans beyond talking,
with warrior cries, sulphuric tears and
with great barrow loads of laughter!
Waiting. Watching: 24–7–365.

Whatever it takes they will give: Breaking the rules. Shaking mediocrity from its cosy little hide. Laying down their rights and their precious little wrongs, laughing at labels, fasting essentials. The advertisers cannot mould them. Hollywood cannot hold them. Peer-pressure is powerless to shake their resolve at late night parties before the cockerel cries.

They are incredibly cool, dangerously attractive inside.

On the outside they hardly care! They wear clothes like costumes to communicate and celebrate but never to hide.

Would they surrender their image or their popularity?

They would lay down their very lives – swap seats with the man on death row – guilty as hell. A throne for an electric chair.

With blood and sweat and many tears, with sleepless nights and fruitless days,

they pray as if it all depends on God and live as if it all depends on them.

Their DNA chooses JESUS. (He breathes out, they breathe in.)

Their subconscious sings. They had a blood transfusion with Jesus.

Their words make demons scream in shopping centres.

Don't you hear them coming?

Herald the weirdos! Summon the losers and the freaks. Here come the frightened and forgotten with fire in their eyes. They walk tall and trees applaud, skyscrapers bow, mountains are dwarfed by these children of another dimension.

Their prayers summon the hounds of heaven and invoke the ancient dream of Eden.

And this vision will be. It will come to pass; it will come easily; it will come soon.

How do I know? Because this is the longing of creation itself, the groaning of the Spirit, the very dream of God.

My tomorrow is his today. My distant hope is his 3D. And my feeble, whispered, faithless prayer invokes a thunderous, resounding, bone-shaking great 'Amen!' from countless angels, from heroes of the faith, from Christ himself.

And he is the original dreamer, the ultimate winner.

Guaranteed!

LFIS Handbook Guidelines

Feel free to use this appendix as a guideline for producing your own similar documents. Don't just copy it! – I know what you are like! Current legislation updates that affect us are pulled together by AMAZE – the association of Christian children's and youth workers. Contact them via www.amaze.org.uk.

Job description for full-time / job-share schools worker

Leeds Faith In Schools offers the services of Christian workers to schools in Leeds to support the curriculum teaching and learning within the Christian module of the RE curriculum. It also provides support to teaching staff in other subjects and departments and in assemblies when invited. The project workers also offer assistance in extra curricular activities such as sports coaching and Christian groups, including occasional residentials. The project is ecumenical, managed by Trustees and the Project Manager, we are active members of the Schools Ministry Network.

1. PURPOSE

To have a face-to-face enabling role in schools so that a Christian presence may be established, maintained and developed there, and to work with others to that end.

2. ACCOUNTABILITY

The worker is accountable to each school in which he/she is working and to the Trustees and Project Manager for all aspects of his/her work. It is essential that the worker is supported by, and accountable to a named person to help them with personal issues and growth.

3. MAIN FUNCTIONS

- *Schools work*: which includes a facilitating and enabling role in local schools living out the gospel through relationships with pupils and staff.
- A *support role* to teaching staff in schools.
- *Liaison work*: which includes establishing relationships with churches and developing and maintaining those contacts.

4. ACTIVITIES

- To be involved in the school community by offering appropriate supportive relationships with individual pupils, school staff and others.
- To contribute to assemblies, lessons and group meetings establishing appropriate aims and objectives.
- To be involved in extra-curricular activities.
- To assist and initiate schools 'Christian focus' weeks as appropriate.
- To support Christian pupils and teachers and other interested adults in Christian outreach in schools.
- To develop ways of linking schools and churches, so that church groups have an active concern for teachers and pupils, and a desire to support schools.
- To develop a relevant programme of residential activities appropriate to the area.

- To report to the Project Manager regularly and attend team meetings.
- To be responsible for effective administration of their work.
- To maintain contact with others involved in youth work in the local area and Leeds as a whole.
- To attend relevant training courses and conferences.
- To undertake personal and professional development.

5. PREFERRED EXPERIENCE AND QUALIFICATIONS

- A committed Christian in sympathy with the aims of LFIS and the Schools Ministry Network.
- Ability to relate well in a school setting, with pupils and adults.
- Ability to communicate effectively with young people and make Christianity relevant and exciting.
- Ability to work in an unstructured setting and to involve others by encouragement, delegation and team building.
- Ability to work alone and also to co-operate as part of an interdependent team.

Please see your Statement of Terms and Conditions of Employment for full details of salary, hours of work and other terms of employment.

Guidelines for schools workers

DO

- Treat everyone with respect.
- Provide an example you wish others to follow.
- Plan activities which involve more than one other

person being present, or at least which are within sight or hearing of others.

- Respect young people's right to personal privacy.
- Have separate sleeping accommodation for leaders and young people.
- Provide access for young people to talk to others about any concerns they might have.
- Encourage young people and adults to feel comfortable and caring enough to point out attitudes or behaviour they do not like.
- Remember that someone else might misinterpret your actions no matter how well-intentioned.
- Recognise that caution is required even in the most sensitive moments, such as comforting a child who is upset.
- Regularly review your work with others.

DO NOT

- Permit abusive youth peer activities (e.g. ridiculing, bullying).
- Play physical contact games with young people in isolation.
- Have any inappropriate physical or verbal contact with others.
- Jump to conclusions about others without checking the facts.
- Allow yourself to be drawn into inappropriate attention-seeking behaviour such as tantrums or crushes.
- Exaggerate or trivialise child-abuse issues.
- Show favouritism to any individual.
- Make suggestive remarks or gestures.
- Rely on just your good name to protect you.
- Believe it could never happen to me.

A Leeds Faith In Schools Associate Worker

- is accountable locally and personally to management group / church / organisation / mentor;
- will meet termly (or half-termly) with LFIS staff and manager;
- is accountable to LFIS for schools work and practice, has access available to all LFIS meetings and trustees if needed and LFIS resource base available free of charge;
- has salaries and expenses paid by primary employer unless authorised by LFIS project manager;
- is required to write *brief* reports for trustees and news-letters when required;
- is responsible for own motivation and structure of work with advice from LFIS to stay within our aims and objectives.

Official conduct

(a) You will maintain conduct of the highest standard such that public confidence in your integrity is sustained.
(b) You must be supported by and accountable to a named person.
(c) No alcohol must be consumed while at work.

Remember that you are working on years of good relation-ships built up in school, and one look, comment or incident could ruin years of work. A 'closed' school is often impos-sible to get back into and ruins most of, if not all, the work done there.

Please read Titus in the Bible to understand about the high standards of conduct expected from Christian leaders.

Appoint leaders in every town according to my instructions. As you select them, ask, 'Is this man well-thought-of? Are his children believers? Do they respect him and stay out of trouble?' It's important that a church leader, responsible for the affairs in God's house, be looked up to – not pushy, not short-tempered, not a drunk, not a bully, not money-hungry. He must welcome people, be helpful, wise, fair, reverent, have a good grip on himself, and have a good grip on the Message, knowing how to use the truth to either spur people on in knowledge or stop them in their tracks if they oppose it. For there are a lot of rebels out there, full of loose, confusing, and deceiving talk. Those who were brought up religious and ought to know better are the worst. They've got to be shut up. (Titus 1:5–11, *The Message*)

Record sheets

NAME:	DATE:

A) Things that went well:

B) Things that didn't go quite as well:

C) Things to develop:

D) People to contact:

E) Things to ask my manager/leader:

ASSEMBLY / LESSON RECORD SHEET

School	Year Group	Assembly title and info	Date

TIMETABLE ENGAGEMENT SHEET

Name: ....   Month ending: ....

	MON	TUES	WEDS	THURS	FRI	SAT	SUN	
Assembly								8am
Lessons								9
								10
								11
Lunchtime								12
Lessons								1
								2
								3
After school								4
Teatime								5
								6
Evening								7
								8
								9
								10pm

Every Child: A Chance to Choose

by Penny Frank

This book is about giving *all* children the opportunity to discover Jesus and to respond to him.

- What do children need to come to faith?
- How can we provide ongoing training for ministers and leaders?
- How can co-operation across the denominations become a reality?

Penny Frank looks at these and other critical issues for children's ministry today. Combining a positive assessment of church resources with a determined effort to trust the eternal promises of God, she holds out the prospect of a ministry that could transform our nation.

'I commend this book by Penny Frank . . . because I believe these pages might help us all to dig beneath our actions and feelings to ask why we are still excluding so many children from the body of Christ.'

James Jones
Bishop of Liverpool